GET REAL
and GET IN

Quoks:
xvii

GET REAL and GET IN

How to Get Into the College of Your Dreams by Being Your Authentic Self

....

DR. AVIVA LEGATT

St. Martin's Griffin
New York

First published in the United States by St. Martin's Griffin,
an imprint of St. Martin's Publishing Group

GET REAL AND GET IN. Copyright © 2021 by Aviva Legatt.
All rights reserved. Printed in the United States of America.
For information, address St. Martin's Publishing Group,
120 Broadway, New York, NY 10271.

www.stmartins.com

Library of Congress Cataloging-in-Publication Data

Names: Legatt, Aviva, author.
Title: Get real and get in : how to get into the college of your dreams by
being your authentic self / Aviva Legatt.
Description: First edition. | New York : St. Martin's Griffin, 2021. |
Includes bibliographical references and index.
Identifiers: LCCN 2021008169 | ISBN 9781250773968 (trade paperback) |
ISBN 9781250773975 (ebook)
Subjects: LCSH: Universities and colleges—United States—Admission—
Handbooks, manuals, etc.
Classification: LCC LB2351.2 .L44 2021 | DDC 378.1/610973—dc23
LC record available at https://lccn.loc.gov/2021008169

Our books may be purchased in bulk for promotional, educational,
or business use. Please contact your local bookseller or the
Macmillan Corporate and Premium Sales Department at
1-800-221-7945, extension 5442, or by email at
MacmillanSpecialMarkets@macmillan.com.

First Edition: 2021

10 9 8 7 6 5 4 3 2 1

For the next generation,
especially Jarron and Micah.

Contents

Part Two
College and Beyond

....

GET REAL
and GET IN

The Impressiveness Paradox

As a former admissions committee member at an Ivy League university, I know a thing or two about what separates the accepted from the rejected. I want to share something important with you, something I don't think you're going to hear from other college admissions officers. It's really counterintuitive, but here it is.

Admissions officers at top universities *know* you're trying to impress us with all that stuff you're doing outside of the classroom. We know that we're *asking* a lot of you. But paradoxically, admissions officers are underwhelmed by students who are clearly managing their lives outside of the classroom in order to impress the committee.

I call it the "Impressiveness Paradox." The paradox is that almost all impressiveness goes out the window when you're *trying* to be impressive.

You know this intuitively in your own social circle. No one is impressed by someone who is trying too hard to make an impression. Like when your classmate shows off their latest selfie on social media, and you know it's totally got a filter. In that situation, it feels like someone trying to "play" you. You know the person is faking.

Exactly the same dynamic applies when admissions officers are sitting around the committee table, making decisions on your application.

There are two main pitfalls in creating your application (and the life you're presenting in the app). The first is not being impressive at all: no clubs. So-so grades. Activities you tried for a semester, then pooped out on. I'm not going to talk about that one. If you care enough about your future to read a book like this, I doubt you're at risk of leaving no impression at all.

However, there's a second pitfall, one you're probably *much* more at risk of falling into (without even knowing it). That's the pitfall of seeming fake. You're overly earnest in your application. You wax poetic about your involvement in the "Earth Club" and make a deadly serious pledge to save every honeybee by graduation. You're not just involved in clubs—you're *president* of every one.

It all smacks of fakeness. There's just no other way to put it.

It's not that we think you're *lying* to us (we can spot the true liars! That's not what we're talking about). But admissions counselors get a feeling when everything has been pre-ordained, pre-managed, and pre-packaged to impress us— which is not impressive.

I want you to avoid this pitfall: that's why I wrote this book. "Getting real" is the first step to getting in and, most importantly, getting what you want out of life.

MY STORY

But before we go any further, I want to share my story.

The year was 2000. I was attending a competitive high school, Princeton High School (PHS) in Princeton, New Jersey. I absolutely loved my experience there, but there was one problem. Everyone who attended was a *rock star*, on and off paper, and it crushed me. Here are the receipts: I went to high school at the same time as Oscar-winning *La La Land* and *Whiplash* writer/director Damien Chazelle (he was class of '03). I also attended school with a now-famous yogi, two future Broadway stars, and several soon-to-be top doctors in the United States. I knew multiple people who got a 1600 on the SAT *freshman* year (without studying . . . or so they said). I spent much of my four years at PHS engaged in deep conversations with brilliant peers whose worldly knowledge far exceeded mine.

While it was an extraordinary opportunity to learn in this environment, I was barely keeping up with my classmates academically, artistically, or extracurricularly. They were in APs; I wasn't. They were in tons of clubs; I wasn't. I wanted to do theater and was fairly talented . . . but I was competing for roles with future Broadway stars and Oscar winners! My dreams seemed meant for them, not me.

At PHS, there was an overarching belief that attending a top college was the *only* way to gain success in life. I didn't grow up with this belief, but it was in the air in my high school and got hammered into me by teachers and classmates.

How did this impact my college plans? I felt I had to

distinguish myself in some way from my classmates. But what could I do? I knew I had to get a head start. So, sophomore year, I selected my first-choice college: New York University.

NYU had a music business program. I was obsessed with Hanson (yes, the "MMMBop" brothers—Google it!) and musical theater—and the music business route seemed like a logical choice at the time. Back then, NYU's music business program was considered one of the best in the country. In the years that followed, I did all I could to make sure I had everything in place for NYU. Test scores at target range: check. Grades good enough: check. Enough "worthy" extracurriculars (or so I hoped): check.

I visited every NYU event I could, taking campus tours, attending information sessions, and going to prospective student gatherings at school. I even asked my dad to contact an NYU professor we knew and visited him at his home. Fortunately, Professor Walter Reinhold, who later became my music history professor, put in a good word for me. I applied for early decision (not knowing how this would impact my family and myself—for example, that it would add quite a bit to my student loans!).

Everything was looking good for my application—at least, as good it was going to look. But the pressure became too much for me in October of 2000. As a high school senior, I got stress-induced pneumonia the month before applications were due. I had to miss several weeks of school and was physically incapacitated for months afterward, not to mention emotionally exhausted.

I barely took time to acknowledge my pneumonia, though

(or the psychological/emotional implications of my illness). I waited and waited for my admissions decision to come in, and when that envelope finally came . . .

BOOM. Accepted. I cried tears of relief, balled up on the floor.

Why did I get accepted? I'll never know for sure, even though I've since served as a member and chair of an Ivy League admissions committee.

But I'm fairly certain that I got into NYU because of my "demonstrated interest" (AKA *obsession* and persistence), alumni connections (I was a triple legacy), adversity (my father became very ill when I was in high school, which probably explains why I was so focused on a brighter future), and my attendance at PHS—a high school that had a good relationship with NYU at the time. My grades and test scores were extremely average for NYU and probably on the lower end of my other classmates who applied.

But all that mattered to me was that *I got in.*

Was NYU *the* thing that made a difference in my life? Did it make me successful today? Maybe my college experience has something to do with my successful career. But ultimately, college was the step that prepared me for the *next* phase of my life. It was not the making of me, nor the end of my story.

As it turned out, my high school experience laid the groundwork for my current career. Did I know *then* that my successes *now* would stem from that four-year period at PHS in which I felt perpetually frustrated and awkward? Um, no!

But with the advantage of time, I can now see how it all fits together. My time at PHS inspired me to go into the field of higher education. PHS got me obsessed with college! My high school experience led to a career of more than 15 years in higher education. In that time I've had jobs in admissions, academic leadership, teaching, and counseling students about how to get into top colleges.

Admission to NYU and any other successes I've had through the years have come because of hard work and luck. There is no secret formula.

Here's what I've learned through my own professional and personal experience and through interviewing the wonderful people you'll meet in this book: *success doesn't go in a straight line*. Rather than create a "perfect" plan for success to be followed no matter what, we must be clear on our own values and goals. Then we can use what happens in life, whether positive or negative, as *fuel* for our next endeavor. Our *mindset matters*—when we keep an open mind and don't force ourselves onto a certain pathway because we think that pathway will make us successful, then we are most able to find true success.

While I could have written a book about how to "wow" the admissions committee by being the best underwater basket-weaving Irish step dancer (just kidding . . . but seriously, that would be a very memorable applicant!), I decided instead to have conversations with widely admired influencers about how college and other turning points affected their lives. Many of their pivotal life moments took place during college, but many moments that paved the way for future success had absolutely *nothing* to do with college. Because, as we'll talk about in this book, your life amounts to so much more than where you go to college.

I asked these leaders for their advice for today's students. They got real with me. And some of their wisdom may surprise you. And guess what? These people may be older than you, but the lessons they share are timeless—and I'll show you the parallels between your story and theirs. Included with these influencers' stories are accounts from students I've coached.

THE PRESSURES TODAY—AND WHY THEY ARE REAL

Here's the thing about high school: it's hard to discover who you really are because there's so little time to actually figure it out. If your life right now is all about the hustle, you're no different than most of my clients. No one is showing you the way—school is teaching you how to get good grades, and your parents are telling you that you need a high SAT/ACT score. Everyone is so worried about hitting specific standardized score benchmarks, essay word counts, and all of those "success metrics." But all these things add up to *not that much* when it comes to getting into college. Even though it may blow your mind to hear it, *grades and SAT scores are not all an admissions office cares about*. Far from it.

If you get nothing else out of this book, I want you to get that.

But right now you, like my stressed-out self from the year

2000, are probably focused on grades and tests. And you're super emotionally vulnerable, too, compared to how your parents and grandparents were feeling when they made decisions about higher education.[1] You feel the stress of your college decision more acutely than anyone around you. They love you and want the best for you—but they're not the ones who have futures riding on this!

Our stress and drive to achieve is not our fault. From the time we're small, we're taught that college is competitive, important, and waaaaaay expensive. If we let them, the financial and emotional pressures can easily overwhelm us.

The struggle is real!

When I was on the Wharton admissions committee, students who were accepted had two things in common: they knew how to do well in school, and they knew how to take standardized tests. Even so, plenty of "perfect" scores were rejected. That's right—we turned away *lots* of 1600 SAT scores. So, unless an applicant's family was donating a mint, there was way more to getting accepted than grades and tests! (College admissions scandal aside, the rules bend a little if your family donates a whole mint. Unfortunately.)

But you still have no idea what it takes to get in, do you? It's not your fault. Admissions officers don't tell you. That means you are probably engaging in a futile guessing game to figure out exactly what admissions officers are looking for.

You pursue a score of extracurricular activities. You add on useless extra courses. You take standardized tests more times than should be legal. All in an effort to "look good" for college applications—while the stress load on you and your parents becomes heavier and heavier.

I'm sure you'd love a book that told you the exact steps to get into an elite college. Unfortunately, I can't give you that book, because—as someone who was involved in selecting students for an elite college, I can assure you—there *are* no exact steps that work for everyone.

And I'm not just saying that because it sounds like the "right thing to say," or to avoid offending any of my former colleagues. My priority here is to help you. I promise you: if there was some magic key, I would tell you. But there isn't, and any book or guru who tells you there is is lying.

But I can tell you this much.

Getting real is the first step on the road to getting in. You showing the admissions committee that you would be an asset to their school has to do with the *authenticity* of your impressiveness.

Admissions committees want to be wowed by you, but they want you to wow them in *your own unique way.* This is great news because it means there's no one way to win.

If you think about it, why would it be any other way? Do you think that colleges want a homogenous bunch of cookie-cutter Stepford students?

Colleges talk nonstop about diversity. Let me assure you: *they really mean it.* Top colleges want a wide range of excellence among the student body, and that doesn't just mean a bunch of people who are great at different academic topics. It means a collection of people who have had unique and varied life experiences—people who have come into their own as young leaders in their own ways, on their own paths. In fact, in some ways that's the very definition of a leader—someone who has cut their own path.

That someone should be *you*.

WHY I WROTE THIS BOOK

I may be framing the college question in a way you haven't considered. You may be in love with a particular brand-name college. (Or maybe your parents are.) Maybe you're a legacy at a prestigious institution, or your friends are all headed to the school 30 minutes from home, so you figure that's the best place for you, too. Maybe you've got your heart set on one school's pre-med program and you just *know* that program is your ticket to success.

But I'm here to tell you this: your college experience is *yours*, and yours alone. You're not living it for your mom or dad or best friend.

I wrote this book because I want you to STOP TRYING TO MAKE AN IMPRESSION and to start living for yourself. I want you to start trying new things and achieving excellence in those things—instead of *running from the possibility of failure*. I want you to avoid spreading yourself so thin that your sense of identity, your values, and your interests get completely lost.

I can help you because I no longer work in an admissions function. Those who do work in admissions can't help you as much as I can. Why not? Because above all, they are looking for *authentic leadership*. If they *told* you what authentic leadership looks like to them—and then you went out and did what they told you in the name of "authenticity"—it wouldn't be very authentic, would it?

Admissions officers are looking for natural leaders. (Not necessarily *born* leaders but young adults who have come to leadership potential on their own.) They want to see how you operate—not how you *perform* when you've been given a paint-by-numbers formula. That's why it's time to stop trying to create a brand that's not you and start being impressive in your own unique and authentic way.

SO WHAT REALLY MATTERS?

Here's a secret I'll let you in on: the priorities of colleges are ever-changing and the politics of admissions are complicated. Know why? It's because *your admission to college is not just about you!*

You read that right.

Your admission is not *just* about you—it's also about how you help the *university* meet its current priorities. It's also, to a lesser extent, about some things you can't control: who your parents are and where you went to high school.

For example: when I attended PHS, over 20 people were admitted to Princeton University . . . out of 275. This is a *ridiculously* high number of people admitted to Princeton from one school! This happened for a few reasons. Number one: "town-gown" relations (PHS and Princeton are located in the same town). Number two: professors' children apply—and when your parents work at a college, your chances of getting in increase dramatically. Number three: an incredibly talented student body (PHS had some of the highest SAT scores in the state and a future Oscar winner or two among us!). Where you went to high school can make a difference in where you go to college—sometimes a big one.[2] But your background does not determine your destiny.

Many of the people I spoke to for this book made individual choices that defied the expectations of their school, communities, or families. These individuals forged their own paths in the world. Their choices were influenced by a variety of circumstances: learning disabilities, family arrangements, and broader cultural events. But each path was unique to the individual, each choice his or her own to make.

Now back to you.

Your success in college and in your career will not be just about "your brand" or the labels you've attached to yourself. In fact, your success has more to do with how you take advantage of opportunities, persist through challenges, and overcome obstacles.[3]

The college admissions process is one of the first tests of persistence. It's not that grades and scores in high school don't matter if you want admittance to a top college—of course they do. You'll definitely need hard work and persistence to meet the very high bar you're trying to reach. Test scores are important: but they are not *all* that's important.

According to the National Association for College Admission Counseling, here's the breakdown on how officers consider your application, from the factors considered "most important" to "least important":

- **Most important**—A student's grades in college prep courses, the strength of a high school's curriculum, the student's SAT/ACT scores, and the student's overall GPA.
- **Moderately important**—A student's essay or other writing sample, activities, recommendations, and class rank.
- **Low–moderately important**—A student's interview with an admissions officer, test scores in the subject the student wants to major in, and student work experience.
- **Low importance**—A student's SAT II scores and portfolios (e.g., art and music samples or other supplements required by the college).

Having a high GPA and good test scores is extremely important: *but that's not enough.* No one, including admissions officers, can predict your admissions results. Each student is unique, and each set of circumstances is unique. Admissions is never as simple as $1 + 1 = 2$.

You can't put all your eggs in one basket. For example: don't focus too much on your GPA and forget about extracurriculars. And once you're out of school, your GPA and test-taking abilities are no longer very important. In the real world, *who you are* and the experiences you've had count for way more.

When it comes to what admissions officers are looking for, your essay and interviews can be two of the most effective ways to stand out from the crowd. Spending time developing your strengths and demonstrating your enthusiasm will take you far—both in getting into the school of your dreams, and in life.

WHAT'S IN STORE

In these pages, you'll listen in on conversations with incredible leaders. You'll learn the mindsets and action steps that people have embraced to start living their authentic lives. Each story can help you build your college admissions candidacy in your own authentic way. The following chapters contain stories from students and professionals, because it doesn't matter when the college story took place! The lessons are timeless and can apply to students of any age. I've interviewed a wide variety of professionals with extremely different life paths because I want you to see yourself in at least one of these stories.

Each story shows you how you can strive to find your authenticity—and avoid the pitfalls of the Impressiveness Paradox. I want to help you achieve the college and career success of your dreams. But this is a participatory process. Each chapter includes reflection questions for you to think about—and then act on. You can begin to apply this book's lessons to your college application process *today*.

While other books offer formulaic advice on how to get a *yes* from the admissions committee, they stop there. What's missing from those other guides are examples of how successful people have managed to find themselves as unique, individual humans—and live authentically. Ultimately, living true to yourself is what will help you win at college and life, beyond grades and test scores.

You owe it to yourself to read this book—because based on my experience in admissions, what you've been doing is probably not going to help you get into your top-choice college. You're likely trying too hard to impress and not doing enough to make an impression. This book will teach you how to live your truth and get where you want to be.

Let's begin.

Some of the exercises within this book and other resources are available for download at http://getrealandgetin.com/.

Part One

CHOOSING YOUR DREAM COLLEGE

. . . .

ONE

Who Am I?

Have you ever asked yourself the question "Who am I?" Unfortunately, you can't answer this question quickly in a superficial, BuzzFeed-quiz kinda way. It's not just a list of the top three things you *like*: "I like Marvel movies, chocolate almonds, and reading." Or a laundry list of things that you *do*: "I've danced competitively for 12 years, I have the highest GPA in my class, and I volunteer with the ASPCA on weekends."

Those qualities are nice, but all they do is scratch the surface of the iceberg that is YOU. Who you *are*—your essence—is about so much more than the "you" you're used to presenting to the world, the you that most of your teachers and friends and classmates (maybe even parents) know.

And I'll be the first to admit—getting in touch with your true self and honoring your unique voice above all others is *hard*. And it isn't another "resume builder" that I'm adding to your to-do list. (I promise.)

So let's start answering this question of "Who am I?"

Rather than doing more, I want you to think back to a time when you did *less*. Think back to when you weren't consumed by the pressures that you're facing today—when you weren't worried about your GPA, going on college visits, or cramming for standardized tests. Find a time in your memory when you were carefree—maybe playing outside with friends at recess in elementary school or hiding under the covers with a flashlight and book long after the time you were supposed to be asleep.

I'm about to ask you to do something that might feel a little silly or immature. But it's actually really important. Just trust me on this and take it seriously. Think back to that little kid— the one who was so excited to be playing, who didn't know the meaning of the word *stress*. What did that little kid get excited about? What was her biggest dream? What put a smile on his face? When she played pretend, what did she play? When they were having the *most* fun, what were they doing?

To get in touch with who we really are, we have to re- connect with that part of ourselves that didn't take on the weight of others' expectations. Remember when life was just about having *fun*—not filling out financial aid forms or stress- ing about your future college major? I know—it seems like it was forever ago! But that little kid is still inside you. Here are a few questions to help jump-start your brain so you can re- connect with that person:

Exercise: When I Was Little

1. When I was little, I wanted to grow up to be _____

_____.

2. That seemed like such a cool thing to be, because __

_____.

3. My favorite game to play was _____

_____.

4. As a kid, I was always _____

_____.

5. What got me more excited than anything was when

_____.

6. What I wanted most of all was _____

_____.

7. I wanted to learn more about _____

_____.

Maybe you're thinking: "What's the point of this? When I was little I was obsessed with the Teenage Mutant Ninja Turtles and I wanted to grow up and be a roller coaster test-rider. How will this information help me get into college?"

I'm going to hit you with two truths. One: life is about a lot more than getting into your dream college, even though this book is designed to help you do just that. College is important—but it is far from everything. Think about it: college represents such a tiny fraction of your life. Four years, a few more if you go on to graduate or professional school . . . that's not a lot of time! Who you *were* as a little kid matters; who you *are* today matters; who you'll *be* when you get out of college (sooner than you can imagine) matters, too.

Which brings me to the second truth: knowing yourself well will set you up for success today, in college, and beyond. So back to the example at hand: let's say you were a Ninja

Turtle–loving, roller coaster–riding seven-year-old whose high-est ambition was to ride every coaster at Six Flags. What can that tell you about yourself? How can the information you learn get you closer to your dream college and a life that makes you feel proud?

Let's follow the breadcrumbs. Did that love of roller coast-ers morph into a love of the outdoors as you got older? Do you like thrills—whitewater rafting, rock climbing, zip-lining? If so—did you know that plenty of colleges provide abundant opportunities for just this type of activity? As you explore col-leges with your future major in mind and look for the program that will set you up well for a career, are you taking into ac-count the social life of the college, what opportunities it pro-vides for *fun*?

Take a deep breath and repeat after me: *college is supposed to be fun!* The college application process may have you guzzling Starbucks and pulling your hair out, but the goal is to find a college where you'll thrive and set yourself up beautifully for what comes next. What's the point of agonizing over where you'll spend the next four years if you don't *enjoy* those four years? *This is higher education, not a prison sentence!*

I've got good news: when you commit to learning more about yourself, there's no bad news to be found. You're not meant to be like anyone else. Maybe you've got certain tapes on repeat in your head: "I'm not athletic enough," or "It's too hard for me to focus, there must be something wrong with me," or "I wish I was more outgoing, like _____" (your sister, best friend, dad). It's all too easy to get caught up comparing your-self to others, or to think you need to be someone else's version of "perfect." Maybe you're thinking: *I don't want to learn more about myself; I'm afraid I'll find out that I'm not enough.*

Know this: you don't have to be like anyone else to be worthy. All those "less-than" thoughts are things that you've absorbed from your culture, your family, your religious com-munity, TV—everywhere—but *where* they came from and how those thoughts got stuck in your head doesn't really mat-ter. What matters is this: *those thoughts aren't the truth.*

Getting in to your dream college is just the beginning—what happens when you're actually there? You're still going to be you, with all of your likes and dislikes and pet peeves and oddball interests. The better you know these things, the more you'll be able to find a college that helps you to live up to your full potential.

The purpose of this book is to help you discover more about yourself, determine which college would be the best fit for your unique personality and talents, and help you set a course to discover what type of work will be exciting for you to do in the world. But in order to figure out what you want out of college and out of life, first you have to know who you are.

What Stories Am I Telling Myself About Myself? Are Those Stories Helping or Hurting Me?

Below is an exercise to help you identify any limiting be-liefs you may have about yourself and to help you move past them.

Not everything we believe about ourselves is true. Want to know if something is true or not? Pay attention to how it makes you *feel*. If it makes you shrink up inside and feel bad about yourself, it's probably not true.

Now: does that mean that there's nothing in your life you can improve upon? Of course not. But there are helpful and unhelpful ways to frame your thoughts. For example: *I'm a slob* is a thought that probably doesn't *feel* good to think or say. A more true thought would be: *Sometimes I procrastinate on cleaning my room, and then I feel anxious when I can't find what I need.*

See the difference between those two statements? One is a negative value judgment; the other focuses on a specific behavior and how that behavior affects you emotionally. Embedded in the second statement is a solution. For instance: you could create a cleaning schedule for your room to avoid the last-minute scramble to find clean socks when you're already late for class.

Now I want *you* to identify unhelpful stories you're carrying around, as well as the negative behaviors that come with those stories . . . because before we can change something, we must first acknowledge why those thoughts are there in the first place.

1. Write Down the Origin Story for the Label or Behavior You'd Like to Change

Let's take, for example, Richard (not his real name). Richard was the "class clown," a label he carried since the sixth grade. Richard enjoyed making his friends and classmates laugh. But he didn't like how he got side-eye every time he tried to step out of his class clown role. For instance: during his junior year, Richard applied for a substantial scholarship sponsored by his town's Rotary Club. He told one friend about going for the scholarship; that "friend" made a snide remark about Richard's academics, questioning whether he was a "serious" enough student to deserve the award. In response to comments like this, Richard had a tendency to be self-deprecating—to call himself things like "dumb but funny" in order to get laughs out of his schoolmates. The result: Richard started to believe his own label and was less and less confident about taking academic risks.

While doing this exercise, Richard journaled about the Rotary Club scholarship and how his friend's reaction had impacted him. After he did, Richard uncovered an origin story for his limiting belief about his intelligence. When he was in sixth grade, he *loved* his social studies teacher and could always make her laugh. But one day, when Richard did well on a test that the rest of the class struggled with, his teacher announced it like this: "I was so surprised to see that *Richard* had the highest grade of anyone in the class!" What should have been a moment of pride for Richard wound up being really confusing. "Surprised—really?" Of course, he kept it to himself.

What behavior(s) are you demonstrating that may give the wrong impression? What stories do you have about yourself that make you feel like crap?

2. Write Down Your Thoughts About the Story

When Richard was asked to identify the story he extrapolated from these experiences, here's what he wrote: "People only like me if I'm making them laugh. They don't take me seriously or believe I can do more than be goofy."

After talking further, it was clear that for Richard, the line between *people* and *himself* was blurry. As a result of the interactions with his sixth-grade social studies teacher and his snide-comment "friend," Richard found that he was less inclined to put himself out there for scholarships. He'd even taken a less-hard math class than the one he was on track for because of fears that the material would be too hard for him. (It wasn't—he found himself helping with friends' homework often.)

Has someone ever called you out as behaving or performing in unexpected ways? How did the interaction make you feel?

3. Name What You're Getting out of the Behavior

While the "dumb but funny" storyline was painful, Richard found himself playing that role more often than not. Why? Richard realized that the "snide comment" friend played a big role; this was someone Richard had been friends with for five years, someone he really looked up to. It was easy for Richard to play into the role this friend had prescribed for him; it was a way of fitting in and holding on to the friendship.

Furthermore, Richard got a lot of gratification out of making his friends laugh, and his "dumb kid" shtick was an easy way to do that. Once Richard saw the subconscious ways he was benefiting from this storyline, the wheels were set in motion: How could he make people laugh *and* do so in a way that allowed him to think highly of himself? Richard didn't want to play the class clown at the expense of his own self-regard.

What emotions do you experience through engaging in this behavior? What behaviors aren't serving you anymore?

4. Choose a New Story—and the Behaviors to Match

To begin changing his perception of himself, Richard wrote a new story. Before, Richard's story had been: *people only like me if I'm making them laugh and don't believe I'm smart.* This story became: *I'm funny AND smart and my friends believe in me.* Then, Richard examined: What friends did he have who encouraged him to be better and reach for more? ("Snide comment" friend didn't make the list—so Richard started spending less time with him.) Richard was able to identify friends and teachers who appreciated his sense of humor and who made *him* feel uplifted—just as he did for everyone around him with his fun-loving ways.

How might you change your story and behavior(s) to better reflect your inner truth?

Work the exercise and get clear on your false stories. It's time to move toward your fullest, most awesome self—those pesky limiting beliefs can take a back seat.[1]

TWO

What Do I Want?

Deciding what you want is completely in your hands, at any point in time in your life. Really. Maybe you think you know what your path *should* be, or you believe that someone important to you expects you to pursue a certain path (whether or not they've said it out loud). Sometimes the signals are unspoken, yet they are so persistent you feel they are coming from you. For instance: let's say we have a boy who lives in a two-parent house and both of his parents are lawyers. Lawyer-boy's parents reminisce about their law school experiences often—that's his picture of college, grad school, and the world of work. Even if Lawyer-boy's parents aren't purposefully pressuring him to follow in their footsteps, Lawyer-boy may have a tough time imagining a different future for himself.

What about you? Maybe *everyone* in your family is a doctor, engineer, or teacher, or went to a particular college or university. How do you draw the line between what *you* want and what others want *for* you? Maybe you've been "strongly encouraged" to pick one university over another, or even pushed toward a particular career track. It's hard to imagine what you've never seen. Do you find yourself following a path because it's expected you'll take it? Or do you truly want it?

The Japanese have the term *ikigai* (生き甲斐). *Ikigai* is a one-word term to summarize your true calling: why you are here on this planet. *Ikigai* is what gets you up in the morning and what drives you when times get tough. In fact, one TED speaker believes that the role of *ikigai* in Japanese culture is one reason why the Japanese have a longer life span than people from any other country.[1]

Your *ikigai* does more than simply reflect your values and beliefs; it's the essence of who you are. Expressing your *ikigai* looks like being your truest self in the world. It's your *real* answer to "What do I want?"

Envision a world where you fully understand your *ikigai*. You discover what you want and you feel at ease in your mind. You gain strength to get through difficult moments en route to your big dreams. Living your *ikigai* brings immense satisfaction and feelings of wellness. When you answer the question of "What do I want?" guided by your *ikigai*, you'll be unstoppable. While your life may be filled with grades, tests, family issues, and friend obligations, don't neglect this important question. The answer you discover holds the key to your best life.

This graphic represents the alignment of *ikigai* around *what you love*, *what you're good at*, *what the world needs*, and *what you can be paid for*.

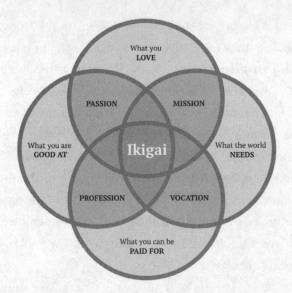

So how do you get in touch with that *ikigai* and start to decide what you want? Go back to the little kid you revisited in chapter one. That little boy or girl thought *everything* was possible. When you were a kid and someone asked what you wanted to be when you grew up, did your answer sound something like "ballerina-astronaut-chef-fireman-actor"? If you were like me, there were no limits to what you could imagine for yourself. "Reality" wasn't a force to be reckoned with—I bet you weren't worried about how much money a ballerina-astronaut-chef-fireman-actor would make! When we get older, we tend to lose our sense of possibility. We think: "It has to be THIS or THIS." While there aren't too many tracks that *actually* lead one to become a multi-hyphenate ballerina, the reality of life is that we can take chances and become many different things. (Psst: Have you heard of Merritt Moore? She's a professional ballerina *and* she has her Ph.D. in quantum physics. So maybe she *will* become a ballerina-astronaut!)

One tactic that could help you discover what you want: build some "buffer time" into your schedule in high school and beyond. I interviewed Broadway producer and elite executive coach Alisa Cohn for *Forbes* magazine. Alisa suggested building in "white space" to your calendar so your greatest creativity can emerge. Your *ikigai* and your creativity are linked, so do what you can to create time for yourself.

If you have buffer time or white space, you won't feel pressure if you haven't picked a major by freshman orientation. You'll have more time to explore and find the major that fits you like a glove—one where you love the material and the people you meet as you're earning your degree.

But what can you be doing *now* to ensure you are finding your *ikigai*? When I coach high school students, I encourage them to take advantage of all the "choice points" in between late high school and the start of college. A choice point is any opportunity you have to explore paths that seem exciting. All of these choice points provide a chance to discover who you are and what you want.

Along the way, you can intentionally expose yourself to different experiences and narratives, whether it's through courses, extracurricular activities, or immeasurable life experiences like taking up knitting. Remember: this is *your* future. You owe it to yourself to explore different paths and choose the one that excites you the most.

Back to our example of the kid with attorney parents. If

he's most excited by a profession in the law—great! There are lots of different career tracks there. He could be a corporate lawyer at a huge firm in a big city. Lawyer-boy could be a civil rights attorney, or a public defender. He could go into family law and help families in crisis. Or, he could be an entrepreneur and provide legal services for small businesses.

But maybe Lawyer-boy decides that law is not for him. Maybe that realization comes as a surprise during his first semester of college. Maybe he knows already that he wants to *stay far away* from the law! How does Lawyer-boy decide what he wants instead? Thanks to his home life, he's got one picture of the world that eclipses all others (i.e., college, law school, attorney life). If Lawyer-boy knows that's what he *doesn't* want . . . how does he discover what he *does* want?

Figuring this stuff out is not easy! You may make a few false starts before you find your way. Remember my story from the introduction? In high school, I thought the music business was THE path for me. Little did I know that I'd be a poor match for the music business field in terms of my personality, the income I desired, and other factors (more on that in part two of this book). As an 18-year-old college freshman, I had no idea that I'd wind up in the career I'm in now.

Remember: 33 percent of college students change their major *at least once*. What's more, one study found that of 3.6 million students who began school at a four-year college, 37.2 percent transferred colleges at least once within six years. Of the students who transferred, *45* percent transferred again![2] After college, the trend holds: by age 35, the average length of each position is less than three years. This means that the average person will hold at least three jobs in the span of less than ten years.[3]

The lesson? You don't need to have everything figured out the day you move into your dorm. But you have to continue to ask the question: What do I want?

Deciding what you want is an ongoing process. College is just a *part* of the process. (A very important part . . . but not all of it.) You may be thinking: if so many people switch their major, change colleges, and can't decide on a career, what's the point of deciding what I want *now*?

Ahem. Ever hear of a thing called *student loans*? While college can be a testing ground for your various interests and potential career paths, it's a very *expensive* testing ground. I want to save you the shock of changing your major three or four times, graduating in six years . . . and coming out the other side with five or six figures in student loan debt. Student loan debt is no joke, for you or your parents; loan debt can cripple your future lifestyle. Choosing the wrong college—or not finishing college while paying the hefty price tag—can affect your ability to eventually buy a house, get married, start a business, have kids, or retire. This means that making the wrong decision can have lasting life consequences.

I've seen it happen—more than once.

This is why it's so important to think about who you are and what you really want *before* you make such a big decision. Now is the time to start considering these things and exploring options. Instead of just picking a brand-name college, think about the student loan consequences and your career goals. Do you *really* need to go to that Ivy League school? Do you need to choose a college based on its *U.S. News and World Report* ranking? In certain fields, you don't need a prestigious degree to make good money after college. In the STEM fields, it can actually work to your advantage to choose a *less* prestigious school. For example, San Jose State University has a regional *U.S. News and World Report* ranking of 22 (a regional ranking is considered a lower-tier group than national rankings in *this publication*). Yet, this university produces many graduates who go on to work in lucrative careers in Silicon Valley. And if you're an international student studying STEM, you can get extra incentives—like three years of legal stay in the United States for entering an in-demand STEM field.[4]

Back to choice points: let's say we have a student named Eliana. Eliana's big ambition is to be a CEO. What choice points can Eliana take advantage of in order to see her big dream more clearly and learn what it would actually take to get that corner office?

Eliana can apply for a summer program that's focused on business ownership and entrepreneurship. Expensive summer programs are not necessary, though. She can also start her own business or a nonprofit using her allowance money and partnering with any connections she may have. Or, she can take a gap year and intern at her family business to get to know the ins and outs of the organization. If there's a college Eliana is interested in, she can introduce herself to the professors and audit a business class or two. Eliana can connect with students in the business program and ask them about their experiences.

If Eliana takes advantage of all these choice points, she's

going to be in great shape when she gets to college. If she still wants to pursue business, she'll know how to pursue it more intelligently. Eliana will maximize her learning by honing in on the specific classes she needs and pursuing extracurricular activities that enhance her understanding of business. But if Eliana finds out she doesn't want to pursue business anymore, she still wins. Now Eliana can think about what she *does* want to pursue and spend time exploring those fields without paying steep tuition dollars toward a degree she doesn't find satisfying.

To get back in touch with that little kid who thought all things were possible, try this exercise, called "Wouldn't it be cool if . . . ?"

Exercise: Wouldn't It Be Cool If . . . ?

For this exercise, let your imagination run wild. For each "wouldn't it be cool if" prompt, write down everything that pops into your mind. Don't be realistic! Let's pretend you get to make up your own reality. Only write a thought down if it makes you smile.

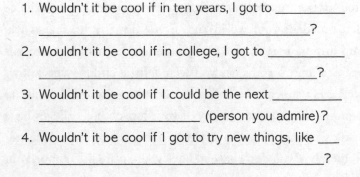

1. Wouldn't it be cool if in ten years, I got to _____
_____?

2. Wouldn't it be cool if in college, I got to _____
_____?

3. Wouldn't it be cool if I could be the next _____
_____ (person you admire)?

4. Wouldn't it be cool if I got to try new things, like ___
_____?

5. Wouldn't it be cool if I could know these people: ___
   _____?

6. Wouldn't it be cool if I became famous for _____
   _____?

7. Wouldn't it be cool if I got to live in this place: _____
   _____?

8. Wouldn't it be cool if I could travel to _____
   _____?

9. Wouldn't it be cool if I could build on this strength I
   already have: _____?

10. Wouldn't it be cool if _____,
    my wildest, BIGGEST dream for my life, came true?

I hope you went BIG on that exercise. If you're using your imagination and creating your dream life, why not make it as fantastic as possible? "Wouldn't it be cool if . . . ?" is designed to get your creative juices flowing. We're taking a look at your deep desires to see if we can follow the stepping-stones to a career you'll find exciting and meaningful, as well as to a fulfilling college experience. Now look at your exercise and work backward.

Let's say you wrote that you'd love to travel to Japan (to study *ikigai*, maybe!). Travel is a deeply enriching experience that broadens your world and, if you do it right, makes you into a more curious and compassionate human. If Japan has been calling to you since you were a little child—who knows why, and who cares?—college could be a great opportunity to explore that interest. Do any of your top-choice colleges have a study abroad program in Japan? How strong is your desire? Remember: you don't have to have your entire life mapped out when you begin college, and you can pursue things you want even if they're not directly tied to your major. So, if you *really* want to go to Japan, how can you make it happen in college?

(Psst: if you want to go to Japan or are itching to have any other travel experience, I say *go for it.* You'll learn and grow so much—and you'll contribute more meaningfully to whichever career path you choose.)

Take a look at the "Wouldn't it be cool if . . . ?" exercise again. If you had to choose your top three desires, what would they be? How could you begin to make your desires reality?

Tuning Out the Noise: How to Cut Through the Clutter of Social Media and Advertising and Get Real About What You Want

I'm interested in you getting in touch with what *you* want—not with what your parents want, not with what the media tells you you want, and not with what colleges tell you you want. You are being inundated every day by messaging and advertising telling you what to like and not like, which experiences you should be craving, which sneakers to purchase . . . and on and on. Being on the receiving end of all that media can be overwhelming. Add to that mix the aggressive marketing tactics of colleges that are hungry for your presence (and, let's be honest, your tuition dollars), and it can all create a cacophony—like people banging pots and pans every direction you turn. All of that noise presents a challenge to you finding your own inner voice and discovering your own desires.

Let's talk for a minute about other people's interests in YOUR college choices. First up, college marketing tactics— which you've probably been on the receiving end of for several years now. In my practice, I've come across many kids as young as *twelve* already being wooed by colleges. These colleges preach the importance of "readiness" and being "competitive." What's the best way to be competitive in the increasingly cutthroat world of college admissions? Sign up the twelve-year-old for college XYZ's summer honors program, of course! (Insert sarcastic sigh.) Here's the truth: those summer programs, while surely valuable and enriching for those who want them, are also big-time money makers for colleges. The marketing messages these colleges send play into your fears that you'll fall behind if you don't attend. They hope you'll pull out your mom or dad's credit card and get your application in, pronto.

What about your high school's interest in your college preparation? You may be in honors classes up to your eye-balls right now. Maybe you were encouraged to overload your schedule with AP and IB classes, all in the name of being "competitive" and "demonstrating rigor" for college one day. But at the risk of what—your health and happiness *now*? High schools with good academic reputations don't al-ways have you as their number one concern. Rather, they are focused on the standards they'd like to uphold, often for marketing purposes on their website or for submitting their own stats to be ranked by their home state or a publica-tion like *U.S. News and World Report*. Simply put, lots of kids in honors classes makes the school look good—thus, more parents want to send their kids there. Bottom line: if you were encouraged to overload your schedule with honors classes, that may be because a schedule full of AP and IB classes is good for the *school*—not for *you*.

Social media can add extra confusion as you seek to get real about what you want. If you're hooked to your phone, chances are you aren't as fulfilled, satisfied, or happy as you could be. According to one study of over 500,000 teens, there is a strong correlation between higher amounts of screen time and depression.[5] It's so easy to forget that the "perfect" lives we're seeing on social media are carefully curated, selected, and filtered. The more time we spend on social media looking at someone else's highlight reel, the more we lose appreciation for the things that are actually pretty great in our own lives. Also, more time on social media means more chances to be bombarded with ads—which can make us *think* we want something that will not actually add value to our lives.

How do we cut through the noise, decide what it is we want, and stay focused (rather than get sidetracked by a million shiny objects)?

One suggestion: put boundaries on your social media time. Maybe you decide that you won't get on social media after eight in the evenings. One of the most productive students I've ever worked with isn't on social media . . . *at all.* He's a volunteer firefighter, works on his family's farm, patented a water filtering device, has launched school publications and clubs, and has taken classes at an Ivy League school. You can do a lot when you eliminate scroll time! If being completely off social media isn't possible for you, how could you set boundaries around your phone usage? What might you do instead of scrolling?

Another suggestion to cut through the noise: have one trusted person with whom you share the stress of the college application process, whom you can count on for sound advice. This should be a person who makes you feel better about yourself—if you don't walk away from this person feeling uplifted, they're not the mentor you need. You read that right! If talking to Mom, Dad, your guidance counselor, your aunt, or anyone else about the college process makes you feel stressed, find someone else to confide in.

A trusted mentor is someone who's not counting on you going to a particular school and choosing a particular major. Your mentor is someone who wants to see you living your best life—that's it. Plenty of people have "suggestions" for you—but often these suggestions are actually hidden agendas. They may want *you* to go to an Ivy League school and major in mechanical engineering because of how it reflects on *them*.

You don't need that kind of pressure! That's why it's so important to confide in someone who doesn't have a horse in the race.

Brainstorm: Who is someone you can talk to about the application process who can help you cut through the noise and hear the truth of what it is you want?

Once you've identified that person, reach out to them. You can say something like this: "Hey, I'm trying to decide between [College X] and [College Y], and I need someone I can bounce ideas off. Would you be free to meet up for coffee?"

Chances are, the person you choose will be honored that you'd include them in this big-time decision. You don't have to make this a big deal or feel weird about reaching out. You owe yourself every possible advantage in the college application process. This is about your future and your happiness—it's okay to decide what you want, name it, and go for it.

I'll be cheering you on.

THREE

Dare to Dream

*The future belongs to those who believe
in the beauty of their dreams.*

—ELEANOR ROOSEVELT

Your future belongs to you and your dreams. No matter your circumstances, you have the power to decide what you want out of life. I want you to look inside yourself—and *then* look around. So many of us do this the opposite way: we look to those around us and base our dreams on what we see others (parents, friends, celebrities) doing. Or we feel the need for validation from others. Often, when a dream is no more than a flicker of a candle flame, we share it with our friends and mentors—and even some people who may not have our best interests at heart. One careless remark from a friend (or stranger!) can be enough to snuff the dream out. We don't give the dream the air it needs to become a roaring fire. Rather than feed the fire and make the dream (and ourselves) unstoppable, we let the flame die.

I believe that your dreams are gifts, and it's your job to

nurture and tend to them and allow them to grow into their fullest forms. When you dare to dream big, you must also protect your dreams. Don't tell them to just anyone—only share your dreams with a select few trusted friends and mentors, the ones who have your back at all times.

What are *your* dreams for college and beyond? We began to get in touch with our dreams in chapter two. Go back and read through your "Wouldn't it be cool if . . . ?" list. Did you think of some more dreams to add to your list? Write them down!

A tip: when you look at your dreams written down, you should feel *excited*—not stressed. When scanning over your list of big dreams and visions, if any one of them sparks stress inside you, cross it out. That item is an *obligation*, not a dream. An obligation is something you do for someone else—your parents, guidance counselor, chemistry teacher, and others. We're getting rid of all obligations and focusing on *you*. The word "should" has no part in your big dreams.

Read that one more time. Maybe you wrote "Go to Harvard" on your list of dreams. A Harvard education is certainly a worthy goal and one to which many people aspire. BUT. I want you to consider why that is on your list and how you *feel* when you look at it. Is going to Harvard *your* dream, or is it a dream that someone else has *for* you? Pay attention to what happens in your body when you look over those words. "Go to Harvard"—does that make you feel expansive or constricted? When you feel expansive, you can't keep the smile off your face. There's a bounce in your step, you breathe easier, and your mind jumps with a thousand possibilities.

When you feel constricted, the opposite happens. You may become short of breath. Your brow furrows. Your brain will tell you all the reasons this will be way too hard, but then you'll try to justify to yourself why this is the right way. This path may feel like the *only* right way—miss it and you're out of luck, take it and you're overwhelmed. Neither option is exciting.

I'm going to ask you to be ruthless with yourself as you move through this book. You're the one who will be living your college experience (and the rest of your life). I want you to continually check in with yourself and ask: "Are the things I *say* I want *actually* what I want?" This is a question you will ask yourself throughout your life—may as well begin now, as you face what is probably your most difficult decision to date. Trust me: this question will serve you well from here on out!

Now that you've written down your big dreams, the question becomes: How will you achieve them? Check out what support you need to get from here to there. Then ask the question: Do I have the support in my life that I need to nurture this dream and turn it into a reality? If not, how can I get that support?

For instance: maybe you will be a first-generation college student. Getting your bachelor's degree will be a *huge* accomplishment in your family—yet you don't want to stop there. You dream about going to graduate school and one day earning your Ph.D.

But it's not safe to talk about this dream around your family. Most of them have a high school diploma—some not even that—and they tease you when you talk about going to college (let alone grad school). How can you get the support you need to realize your big dreams?

Well, you could start by sharing your dream with a trusted teacher or guidance counselor who can lay out what the path to a Ph.D. would look like. Go on the internet and see: is there anyone near you who has a story similar to your own? Earning a Ph.D. seems so far out of reach—until you meet someone who's done it. Can you find someone on the other side of your goal who could give you advice? Even better if that person comes from a family situation similar to your own.

Don't be shy in reaching out and asking for the support you need. Make no apologies about nurturing and protecting your dream and find those who are one hundred percent on board. With the right support, you'll begin to see that *anything* is achievable.

Any dream you choose to pursue is worthwhile—as long as you know the *why* behind your choice and feel excited about pursuing it. In this chapter, we'll meet people who had the audacity to follow their wildest dreams, even amid doubts and unknowns. These people are now living dreams that once seemed impossible—even to them. That can be your future, too.

. . . .

Adam Grant: From Harvard Dreamer to New York Times Bestselling Author

Today, Adam Grant is the author of five books that have sold millions of copies. He's been Wharton's top-rated professor for seven straight years(!). In 2016, he received a standing ovation for his TED talk, which has been viewed over 17 *million* times.[1]

But before all that, Adam was just a kid from Michigan. Adam grew up just outside Detroit—almost everyone he knew ended up attending the University of Michigan or Michigan State. Both are great schools within driving distance of his boyhood home. Adam figured he might end up there, too. It's what was expected and where his friends were going.

But staying in Michigan wasn't Adam's dream.

Adam provides a powerful example of someone who followed a dream—quite literally! Adam first grew excited about the dream of going to Harvard when his unconscious mind expressed itself in his sleep. Says Adam: "In September of my senior year of high school, I woke up one morning and I had a dream that I went to Harvard. The dream felt real; I woke up thinking that I was going to Harvard. That day when I got home from school, I started working on a Harvard application."

Adam took immediate action, no matter how impractical applying to Harvard may have seemed to those around him. He nurtured the dream before anyone had the chance to tell him it was ridiculous and talk him out of it.

Adam ended up applying to Harvard, several other Ivy League schools, and the University of Michigan and Michigan State (just in case). He got into Harvard Early Action, sent in his acceptance the next day, and withdrew all his other applications. Just like that, his dream (literally!) became reality.

Once Adam got to Harvard, his journey to explore his intellectual, personal, and professional interests didn't end. At the end of his freshman year, he decided to stay in Boston for the summer. In order to do so, he had to get a job and needed to find a way to pay for school because his financial aid ran out. The first job he interviewed for rejected his application. His second interview, which was at Let's Go Publications, didn't go too well, either. Adam had so perfectly crafted his answers to what he *thought* the interviewers wanted to hear that he came off sounding like a robot. (He should have read this book first!) Adam's interviewer asked him if he'd ever been in the military—so precise were his answers! Ultimately though, Let's Go Publications hired Adam. (According to Adam, they were desperate.)

Working at Let's Go Publications was a big job, and Adam had little related experience. He had to act fast and learn on the job. When he first started, Adam even violated the terms of his contract, granting refunds to clients who had paid for ads in the Let's Go travel guides the previous year. Adam says he was the first employee in the history of the company to ever *lose* money that was already on the books.

This initial setback gave Adam serious doubts about his abilities and fit. Says Adam: "I told my mom I was thinking about quitting. She said, 'I didn't raise a son to be a quitter. You work at that job until they fire you.' She was laughing but she said, 'You really have to give this a shot.'"

Adam stayed with it. He began to apply what he was learning in his psychology classes, where he was reading, for example, the book *Influence: The Psychology of Persuasion* by Robert Cialdini. He started to think of the job as a challenge: How could he succeed in the position using the stellar Harvard education he was receiving? Adam eventually improved in the job and sold the largest advertising package in Let's Go Publications' history. He was promoted the next year.

This experience led to Adam's eventual career path. He began to wonder how organizations could utilize psychology for their benefit. For instance, how could businesses do a better job hiring and motivating people? Adam decided he wanted a job where he could think about these questions full-time.

Adam did not fully master the Let's Go Publications job at first, but he dove into his responsibilities while taking opportunities to learn along the way. His mindset, persistence, and willingness to learn ultimately led him to success—he was eventually promoted to director of advertising. Ultimately, this experience inspired Adam's choice to build his expertise in management and organizations, which is what he's known for today.

You can follow the lessons in Adam's story to pursue your own dreams and to positively transform your life:

- **Take the road less traveled.** When everyone in your town is going to Michigan or Michigan State (or your local college), consider whether or not that is the right path for you. Really take time to look at what options are available to you and how these options fit with your academic, career, and personal goals.
- **Choose a college community that "gets" you.** Says Adam on choosing Harvard, "I loved the idea of being in a place where intellectual curiosity was seen as cool instead of dorky." For you, what does that ideal

college community look like? It may include a bunch of dorks, a bunch of jocks, an abundance of tech nerds, or something else completely different.

- **Think about more than just the academics.** Adam was a competitive springboard diver; he also wanted to be able to drive home from college if needed. Two of the reasons Adam was drawn to Harvard were its location and its diving coach. Not all of your ambitions around college have to be related to your future major. When you think about how you'd like to spend your time in college, what lights you up and brings you energy? You may choose to pursue extracurriculars that are intellectual, creative, or athletic. College provides hundreds of these opportunities; think about how you'll enrich your life outside of the classroom.

- **Apply creativity and curiosity in the face of challenge.** After messing up big time, Adam reframed his perspective on the Let's Go Publications job. He was on the verge of quitting—but instead of giving up, Adam made his job a game. He wanted to see how he could make the job a "challenge" instead of a lost cause. You too can re-imagine and change the way you experience difficulty by applying creativity and curiosity.

. . . .

Client Story: Jennifer's Dream to Make a Difference

Just like Adam, my client Jennifer is a big dreamer and high achiever. During her high school career, Jennifer studied and became fluent in both Arabic and Spanish. She was an accomplished public speaker, gaining awards in moot court and mock trial. In class, Jennifer maintained a 4.0 GPA while taking advanced placement classes such as calculus, multivariable calculus, computer science, statistics, biology, chemistry, physics, and both micro- and macroeconomics. (She's no slouch!) By senior year, Jennifer had exhausted her high school's available advanced mathematics courses and had begun taking math at Harvard University.

But outside of class, Jennifer's first motivation—her real dream—was to positively impact others' lives in whatever endeavors she pursued.

Early on, Jennifer founded a business leadership club at her high school. Through this club, Jennifer brought in speakers to educate the student body on STEM-related business topics. But that wasn't all; in her junior year, Jennifer expanded the club to become an interschool business organization and onboarded a dozen industry partners. Thousands of lives were impacted through these STEM education programs that all started with Jennifer's dream. Even more impressively, Jennifer patented a safety device that prevents drunk driving and co-founded a student connection portal app.

Even though Jennifer accomplished a lot in high school while being a rock-solid student, she was still unsure of her intended major. And that's totally okay. Jennifer was focused on pursuing her dreams and impacting lives . . . not on developing some kind of packaged strategy to perfectly fit a major and college. As her advisor, I helped Jennifer reflect on the merits of potential career paths before we started the college application process. Jennifer decided that innovation, technology, and business were her top passions. She ultimately decided to apply early decision and was accepted into the University of Pennsylvania's prestigious Management & Technology Program, which will earn her a dual degree in business and in engineering.

Why did Jennifer get in? In reality she would have been a competitive applicant to many colleges (but not *every* school, just the best-fit ones). You can be, too. Here are lessons from Jennifer that you can apply to achieve excellence in and outside of the classroom—in your own way.

- **Take rigorous courses (appropriate to you).** You have to challenge yourself to be the best you can be. Jennifer didn't take hard courses in every single subject, and you don't have to, either. But you want to focus on excelling in the subjects where you're especially strong (as Jennifer did in math—exhausting her high school's math curriculum and taking a Harvard college course). Really take time to look at the course options available to you and how these courses fit with your academic, career, and personal goals.
- **Be a self-starter and self-driver.** No one was telling Jennifer which activities to select. She chose the activities that truly interested her and dove into them deeply. Being driven by her own interests allowed her to achieve her maximum potential. Thousands of lives were ultimately changed because of her business club, entrepreneurial endeavors, and volunteer work. Even if you're impacting one life at a time—through

babysitting your sibling, providing great customer service at your local Target, or filing papers at your internship—you can do your work with purpose and intentionality in order to make the opportunity (and you) as great as possible.

- **If you have a lot of interests, spend time reflecting on how you want to focus your college application process.** Jennifer wore many hats. She could have gone the foreign language or speech and debate route as a language studies major, or she could have been a traditional engineering or business student. (Or something else completely different!) But ultimately, Jennifer's application process reflected her top interests. The stories Jennifer shared in her application essay highlighted these interests. Once she gets to college, Jennifer may decide to explore a number of different paths. However, focusing and honing in on her strengths helped her stand out to her chosen university.

Jennifer and Adam are not outliers. While their accomplishments are unique to them, their success-oriented mindsets are available for anyone to adopt. Each had a dream and took steps to turn that dream into reality. In Adam's case, the dream of going to Harvard was immediately clear. In Jennifer's case, she and I worked together to refine her vision and dream. *Both routes are perfectly fine.* If you have a big dream that's screaming at you—great! Go all in! If you have to do some digging and polishing to uncover your dreams and identify specific ambitions and paths—that is great, too. Don't worry if your dreams are not immediately clear to you, as Adam's dream was to him. Just continue to ask yourself the question: What excites me? Know that your path is not meant to look like anyone else's; continue to follow your interests, and you'll be on the path to your dreams.

REFLECTION QUESTIONS

- Write down your dream colleges. Throw self-imposed limitations out the window. Underneath each one, write down a little about *why* that college would be a dream to attend.
- Have you ever had a dream that seemed impossible come true? Why was it so exciting to you? What was amazing about how the dream came to be? Write about the experience.
- Write down a challenge you're facing—either at school, at your job, or in a relationship. How can you change the way you think about it or the way you approach it?

Values Check

Always remember that it's not about finding the "best" college—it's about finding the best college *for you*.

I've introduced you to some amazing people who forged their own best college path. Now I want to give you super-practical advice on ways you can find the right college for you. Below are five questions you can ask yourself when scouting colleges. They're designed to help you learn about an institution's values and priorities. Do they match up with your own?

For instance: Let's pretend you're interested in going to Carnegie Mellon's Tepper School of Business. You owe it to yourself to do some research:

Question 1: What is the college's culture and character?

Head over to the university's "about" page on their website and check out headings like "Our Mission and Vision" (or something similar). A school's mission statement is likely to be several paragraphs long, but you might find one sentence that summarizes it.

The Tepper School of Business mission/vision reads like this: "The Tepper School of Business is committed to improving the critical thinking and leadership capabilities of individuals so as to enhance their value to business and society." (That's a bit dry, but hey—it's for a business school!)

The motto is a short phrase or saying that captures a school's history, character, and culture. It provides a sense of the school's values and educational philosophy. Carnegie Mellon University's motto is "My heart is in the work."

For me, this phrase suggests that we can't separate the core of who we are from what we do. Does this sound like you? Perhaps you're more philosophically minded and believe we're a lot more than the work we end up doing in the world. If a school's motto doesn't align with your own internal compass, it may be best to choose a different school.

Question 2: What are the college's strategic goals for the next few years?

Look for the university's published strategic plan. This document announces an intention to support that plan with resources and, most important for you, with students who can take advantage of those resources. Some college presidents may be looking to enhance community engagement while others may be looking to advance global opportunities. For Carnegie Mellon and Tepper, key priorities are to "foster innovation and to use data for social good."

This means that Tepper may be interested in students who have launched a nonprofit, have worked with big data, or are highly engaged in volunteer work. Does that align with the work you've been doing throughout high school?

If so, awesome! You can wow an admissions professional by showing them you understand the link between your passions and experiences and the school's stated goals. Conversely, the school can provide you with resources, opportunities, and academic programs to take you to the next level.

Question 3: What are the academic choices and how are they structured?

Does the school use block scheduling (scheduling short but intensive classes) or traditional semesters? Does the school emphasize a core curriculum or their lack of a core curriculum? What about the subject you're interested in— what kind of research are students and faculty doing within this program?

Think about what you might like to major in and check out those academic programs. Would going to school XYZ adequately prepare you for a future in that field?

At Tepper, there are ten concentrations to choose from. The faculty hope students "enhance their skills in quantitative and analytic reasoning," and the school aims to "provide the social, economic and political context for understanding business decisions in a global environment." If numbers, data, and the influence of external forces on business decisions fascinate you, Tepper might just be the place for you.

Question 4: What college-based initiatives are being funded through donations?

A more to-the-point way to ask this: Where's the money?

Knowing where the money is flowing indicates where school priorities are today or where they may go tomorrow. You can check this out for yourself via press releases on college and university websites. You can also investigate the *Chronicle of Philanthropy* at philanthropy.com. Check out the academic areas of interest to you. Has your potential program just received a big fat wad of cash? More money means more opportunities—maybe for scholarships, cool new study abroad programs, improved facilities, and more.

Let's look at Tepper again. The Tepper family gave two BIG donations in the last 20 years: they donated $55 million in 2004 and $67 million in 2013. Since these donations were received, the school has expanded its facilities and strengthened its global reputation.

You want to know if the school "puts its money where

its mouth is," that is, funds the initiatives they claim to care about. Conversely, if your potential college is donating to causes and programs that go against your core values, you don't want to find out about it midway through your first semester.

Question 5: What connections and relationships can you build with alumni, current students, administrators, and professors of the college?

Establishing contact with people associated with the college can give you a personalized look at life inside. You can get a sneak peek to help you determine if said college is really right for you.

Don't know where to find alumni? A quick online search can yield tons of potential contacts. Check out regional alumni groups listed on the college's website; see if there are any alumni you're connected to through your high school or through social media. Find someone who seems nice and ask if you can give them a call. Or better still, meet for coffee. Going on informational interviews with alumni will give you a sense of what college life is like and how your interests might fit with the opportunities said college offers. But don't stop with alumni! Go on campus visits or attend summer programs. Talk with administrators, current college students, and professors.

Establishing relationships like this will help you identify what elements of the college might fit with your interests. And it doesn't hurt your chances of getting in. Ever heard "it's not what you know, it's who you know"? (There's a whole chapter on that later in this book!) The more relationships you build with people associated with the college, the more people you have invested in the fate of your application. AKA, you'll have more people pulling for you—always a good thing!

FOUR

Break the Family Mold

It is never too late to be who you might have been.

—GEORGE ELIOT

Regardless of where you are in the college application process, the first thing you need to think about is YOU: Your priorities and goals. You may think the college process is all about molding yourself to whatever the college or grad program wants you to become—that elusive "perfect" applicant. But as you'll soon see, there *is* no perfect applicant. In college admissions and in life, you just play to your strengths and find ways to develop yourself into the best version of yourself.

Think back to my client Jennifer, whom I introduced in the last chapter. As well rounded as she already was, Jennifer could have put even more pressure on herself to "build out" her weaknesses. She could have chosen to pursue AP literature and history classes so that she appeared across-the-board stellar to college admissions officers.

But Jennifer (wisely) chose to build on her strengths. She was already so well equipped in math and science: Why dilute her strengths in order to present a "perfect" façade, especially given that she didn't plan to pursue a career in the humanities? Jennifer would have hurt her chances of getting into her dream college if she were more concerned about checking boxes than capitalizing on her strengths. So will you. Admissions officers want to know *you*; if you're playing the role of "perfect applicant," they'll be able to tell. You'll end up stressing out needlessly and possibly self-sabotaging.

Knowing yourself and playing to your strengths is easier said than done. For instance: What if *everyone* in your grade is taking AP physics, and you feel tempted to sign up for the class, too? Problem is, you don't really want to: you already have a full and challenging class load, the class is notoriously difficult, and a solid understanding of physics isn't needed for your future career goals.

It takes courage to go against the flow—to decide what's best for you and to stick to your truth. In chapter three, we met Jennifer and Adam, who did just that. In this chapter, we'll talk about the courage it takes to break the family mold: to chart your own path, believe in it, and see it through—even if the path is different than one your family has in mind.

Ever heard the quote at the beginning of this chapter? Mary Ann Evans was a leading Victorian-era writer whose work you might read in your English class under her pen name: George Eliot. Evans took on a pen name to protect her identity and overcome the stigma of being a female author in a time when women were second-class citizens. But breaking the family mold is just what she did: Eliot pursued and attained a formal education (not typical for women of the time) and eventually questioned her faith, which almost caused her family to disown her. Despite the pressures of her family and of society telling her what she *should* be, Eliot persisted in her writing career, becoming an author whose work has been read across centuries.

Eliot followed her own intuition in order to achieve her dreams in a time when breaking from prescribed social patterns made her an outcast. Today, for most of us, the price of taking a different path is not so steep (thank goodness). You too can access your own intuition and let it guide you in the path to your dreams. In fact, following your intuition is *exactly* how you can become competitive in the college application process. The earlier you start thinking about (and more importantly, *acting on*) your interests, the more impressive you'll be to college admissions officers.

Following your intuition and breaking the family mold means trying new things and even disappointing people along the way. Will there be difficulties as you chart a course separate from your loved ones? Yes. But the risk is worth it. Playing it safe and doing the same thing as your peer group or family may seem tempting, but as the saying goes: "no risk, no reward." Going your own way will help you impress college admissions officers. More importantly, you will gain practice in honing your intuition and taking action—skills that will serve you well for the rest of your life.

REFLECTION QUESTIONS

1. What stigmas exist in your family? These could be career related (maybe your family looks down on certain colleges and career paths) or not (maybe your family talks negatively about people who live in a certain state). Whatever stigmas you've been exposed to, write them down so you can see the thoughts and evaluate your own feelings toward them.

2. What stigmas exist at your high school? Is a certain type of college seen as the *only* acceptable one, while others are derided? Write down the biases of your peer group and teachers so you can evaluate them.

3. Can you think of other instances of negatively biased thinking you encounter in your environment (place of worship, friend group, social media, etc.)? Write them down.

4. How do these stigmas shape your worldview? Are you surprised by anything you wrote down—for instance, did you discover you have a negative opinion that is not actually based on fact or your own experience?

It can be alarming to see all the negative beliefs and biases of other people that *we* are carrying around, too.

Awareness is the first step toward unburdening yourself of others' prejudices.

Going against the pattern your family has established is difficult—but plenty of others have done it. So can you. In this chapter I will introduce you to Henry Louis Gates Jr., someone who has defied the circumstances of his upbringing and built an AMAZING life for himself. I'll also provide you with reflection questions to consider if *you* are your most significant obstacle in the college application process—and how to overcome it.

The better you know yourself, the easier your decisions become. That's why this chapter concludes with questions for reflection as well as a personal meditation meant to help you consider your background, identity, and the strengths you offer the world.

So let's begin, shall we?

· ·

Henry Louis Gates Jr.: Taking Advantage of a Societal Moment of Change

Henry Louis Gates Jr. broke away from the traditions of his family after seeing an opportunity he had previously never considered. His family had a tradition of attending one type of university, yet Henry was captivated by the possibility of attending the Ivy League and eventually made that dream a reality (despite setbacks). Often, we *think* we know what our path will be—until another option is presented that suddenly captures our imagination. It is an act of courage to break with the traditions our family has established *and* with our own preconceived notions of which path we should follow.

Today, Henry Louis Gates Jr. is the Alphonse Fletcher University Professor and director of the Hutchins Center for African and African American Research at Harvard University, a MacArthur Genius, an Emmy Award–winning filmmaker, and producer and star of PBS's *Finding Your Roots* (among many other titles and accolades). Yet the Ivy League was a far cry from his humble West Virginia origins, where Henry developed an interest in ancestry and genealogy.

"When I was nine, the day after my grandfather's funeral, my father showed me his father's scrapbooks," said Gates. "In one of those scrapbooks, there was an obituary of my great-great-great-grandmother Jane Gates, who died January 6, 1888, and it was 'Jane Gates: An Estimable Colored Woman.' She had been a slave, and my grandfather never wanted us to forget her. That night I looked up the meaning of the word *estimable* and said, 'Wow, she's estimable! I must be estimable, too!'"

Family and tradition were very important in Gates's family. All of his older cousins went to the historically Black universities Howard, Morgan State, or Bowie State—but when Henry applied to college in the 1960s, the civil rights movement was in full swing. His generation sought to integrate universities, so Gates never really considered attending a historically Black college (or HBCU). After attending an Episcopalian church camp in 1965 and seeing the mostly white kids all planning to attend Harvard, Princeton, and Yale, Henry decided that was what he wanted, too.

"I applied to Exeter [high school] because the coolest kid

at the church camp had gone, and I went there in '67," Henry recalls. "But I was so homesick that I came home and graduated from Piedmont High School."

Henry's homesickness was understandable. In 1967, there were no cell phones. Henry couldn't FaceTime with his mom and dad, or keep up a constant text thread with his friends back home. About 800 miles separate West Virginia and New Hampshire (where Exeter is located), but for Henry the two places must have felt like they were on opposite sides of the planet. Air travel was prohibitively expensive in the sixties—so once Henry was in New Hampshire, he was *there* for the duration of the school year. A world away from home, surrounded by faces that didn't look like his, without technology to keep him tethered to his community—it was all too much.

Yet when Henry came back home, he felt he'd made a mistake. At Exeter, Henry had been a breath away from the Ivy League, the dream that he had nurtured since his days at camp. Back in West Virginia, he was suddenly a world away from that dream—again. In an act of vulnerability, Henry screwed up his courage and asked Exeter for readmittance for a postgraduate year just so he'd have a better chance at his dream schools (would *you* be willing to delay college for a year—all your friends are having exciting freshman experiences, and you're the oldest person in high school?).

Exeter said *no*. That's it—dream over!

But Henry's path to the Ivy League wasn't finished.

Henry went to a local junior college for two years, then to West Virginia State University. His brother had gone there, so it was familiar. Henry got straight As in his first semester and decided to write a letter to Yale. They told him to apply; he did.

And he got in. Henry transferred to Yale during his sophomore year.

Despite the disappointment of Exeter barring the door, Henry worked up the courage to make the "big ask" of Yale. I'm sure the sting of Exeter's *no* was still with him, even two and a half years later. But Henry knew that *no* can sometimes mean *no for now* and that you miss 100 percent of the shots you don't take.

Henry had realized his dream of attending the Ivy League— but that doesn't mean that actually *living* the dream was easy. Henry had a major case of impostor syndrome when he arrived at Yale. "When I got there, I thought that everybody would be Albert or Alberta Einstein, and I just didn't know," said Henry. "I was excited and terrified. I was humbled to be there, but there was no question: I was going to give it a try. The last thing my father said before I left home was, 'If they don't treat you right, come on home.' That was very liberating to me." Henry wasn't counting on Yale to be his *only* route to success.

But the longer he stayed at Yale, the less he wanted to come home. Henry liked the university right away. His junior year, Henry was accepted to Phi Beta Kappa, and he graduated summa cum laude. Henry describes the fit between him and Yale as "magic."

This "fit" provided the launching pad for the rest of Henry Louis Gates's career. From being enamored yet intimidated

by the Ivy League, to becoming a well-loved and widely respected Ivy League professor himself—Henry Louis Gates
Jr. has come a very long way. But his path didn't move in a
straight line. He dealt with closed doors and unexpected de-
tours. Yet, Henry came to realize his dream through going
off-road and through the back door.

But once he passed through, he didn't stop walking.

Henry did not achieve success just from luck and intelligence. He worked hard, he maneuvered when things didn't go
his way, and he kept true to himself as he pursued his goals.
What can you borrow from Henry and apply to your own life
situation?

- **Don't give up if you don't get in the first time.** If
  you want that Ivy League school—or *any* school, for
  that matter—and it doesn't work the first time, try
  another way. This could mean you join the military
  and return as a veteran, or you could take on a 3+2
  engineering and liberal arts program. (Never heard
  of this? It's a dual-degree program that allows you
  to spend three years at a liberal arts college and two
  years at another college in an engineering program.
  You get the benefit of a liberal arts degree as well as
  a highly technical degree: a certified credential in
  both "hard" and "soft" skills.) For example, Columbia University Engineering partners with many liberal arts colleges to enable students to obtain their
  engineering degree through Columbia. You could

also take an impactful gap year (or years) and then
apply again.

- **Use an emotion, a characteristic, or your "roots"
  as your anchor as you chase your dreams.** Henry's
  family history, especially his relative who was en-
  slaved, served as a guidepost for how he wanted to
  set his goals. His "estimable" relative gave Henry
  inspiration for the kinds of qualities he wanted to
  embody, even if he didn't have an exact career direction in mind. Henry built on his family's legacy by
  honoring his roots while taking a different path ed-
  ucationally and professionally. Who in your family
  would you like to emulate? You can look to someone
  living or deceased!

- **Examine all your reasons for your specific desires.**
  For Henry, going to an Ivy League school instead of
  a historically Black college was an important symbolic
  cultural choice at that moment in history. Think about
  the significance of your college choice in your own
  context. Are you first in your family to go to college?
  What is the meaning of your choosing a certain school
  or major? Get a bigger picture of how your choice impacts those around you and how it plays a role in your
  larger world. For example, how might the outcome of
  the 2020 U.S. election shape your view of the country and what opportunities you can make for yourself?
  If you can connect your dreams to something larger
  than yourself, you'll likely be more inspired to persist
  in them—even when the going gets tough.

Like Dr. Gates, do you envision that someday you want to make a mark on the world in a distinguished way? If so, you'll definitely want to get to know one of *Fortune* magazine's World's 50 Greatest Leaders in 2018, Michael Sorrell, who is one of the most decorated college presidents in the United States. Read more at www.getrealandgetin.com.

· ·

Client Story: When Going Against Authority Figures Looks Like a Really Bad Idea (From the Outside)

Henry Louis Gates Jr. has a long track record of success after breaking away from his prescribed path. By contrast, people like my client Bethany are at the beginning of their stories and careers. But Bethany has already achieved greatness and is well on her way to achieving even more—and she's done it by having the courage to follow her own instincts and break with the advice she was given.

Bethany attended high school in Illinois, where she carried an almost-perfect GPA. Bethany was an exceptional student in that she managed to balance her many extracurricular involvements and excel academically while coping with chronic illnesses. These illnesses forced her to miss school and get behind on assignments. Bethany's energy dipped during certain times of the year, which made staying on top of her coursework a challenge. Bethany's doctors suggested that she cut back academically and extracurricularly in order to best manage her illnesses.

But Bethany knew that taking care of herself meant tending to her own ambitions. Bethany worked as a liaison for her local Red Cross and later served as the group's vice president.

She was active in the robotics club at her high school and was captain of the debate team. Bethany was a co-founder of her school's DECA (a not-for-profit career and technical student organization) chapter, where she held various roles, including those of publicist, treasurer, and president of fundraising. She was also a team captain for a major foundation related to the illness that she suffers from.

Bethany's extracurricular hours were packed, too. Bethany worked as a teacher's assistant at a tutoring company, completed an internship at a law office, volunteered at her local library, and served in an organization that supports people living with Alzheimer's disease. While fulfilling these roles, Bethany acquired skills in event planning, fundraising, and financial management. But more than these skills, Bethany cultivated a mindset that would enable her to balance her personal challenges with her unyielding ambition.

Bethany demonstrated tremendous grit: she maintained a high GPA and invested many hours into her extracurricular activities, all the while living with her illness. Rather than seeing her illness as a liability, Bethany chose to appreciate the unique lens on the world that life with chronic illness offered her (even with all its challenges). For her Common Application essay, Bethany wrote about her personal challenges and her ability to face them. Bethany was accepted to NYU, where she is now a flourishing member of the student body.

Bethany's story is unique, and I'm not advocating working at the expense of your health and happiness. What we can learn from Bethany is the gift of knowing yourself inside and out. Bethany beautifully balanced the tension of life with illness and her own ambition: these two elements of her experience were not mutually exclusive, and each informed the other. Sometimes going for your dreams means persevering in the face of difficulty, even if those around you don't understand what's driving you. It's hard to stick to your vision, especially when others are taking the easy road! Bethany stayed true to her vision despite authority figures asking her to scale back her dreams—and the payoff was huge.

How can you take a page from Bethany's book as you work toward your big dreams?

- **Adopt a "no excuses" mindset.** Bethany's doctors advised her to take it easy and to scale down her workload. Instead, Bethany deployed her creativity and worked with her school in order to make up assignments that she had to miss when her illness flared up. Rather than look at her situation as either this or that (she could exacerbate her illness by working too hard *or* scale down her ambitions and loosen her grip on the future she dreamed about), Bethany found a third way: she could maintain her commitments while honoring the physical limitations imposed on her by illness. By taking this third way, Bethany was able to complete assignments *and* take on leadership roles. If you live with illness, how can you honor your body and do the things you dream of? Are there supportive adults who can accommodate you as you seek to do both?
- **Take care of yourself.** While I would never advise going against doctor's advice, Bethany knew herself

better than her doctor knew her. Bethany pursued her goals of having the best possible life with her friends and making an impact on the world. If she hadn't pursued those goals, the non-action would have taken a psychological toll on Bethany. Honoring your ambitions and pursuing your goals are parts of a healthy life, just like eating healthy food, drinking enough water, and getting your flu shot. Achieving goals gives you a sense of purpose and happiness, which is hugely important to a healthy body. One of the ways that Bethany takes care of herself is by choosing to focus on what's most important to her.

- **Give back to your community.** One of Bethany's most meaningful activities was her role as team captain for the foundation benefiting those affected with her illness. Bethany didn't get to choose to be sick—yet she used her experience with this illness to benefit others through raising money in the search for a cure. When you're thinking about your own extracurricular activities, how can you use a difficult experience as an opportunity to give back, contribute, and maybe even help others to heal? When we help others who are going through situations similar to our own, we get to experience gratitude for our past difficulties.

REFLECTION QUESTIONS

Review your own background and experiences:

- Who is helping you decide your college path? List the names of the person or people who are helping you with this decision.
- Is there an "expected" path one (or all) of these people believe you'll take? If so, write it down.
- Now: How do *you* feel about this expected path (if there is one)? Is it aligned with the future you see for yourself?
- If the expected path is not what you want, how would you begin to step off it? List concrete steps here, such as: "Have a conversation with Dad to tell him I don't want to go to _____." (I know this may be scary! The goal here is to get the action steps written down. Even if you have a fear response, just get them on paper. You can take the action later.)
- What challenges do you face in your application process? (Challenges may include: life with a chronic illness, lack of knowledge about the application process, limited financial resources for college, etc.)
- What is your most *significant* challenge?
- What actions could you take to overcome that challenge? (For instance: if your main challenge is the financial burden of college, maybe you could meet with your school counselor and have her walk you

through the Free Application for Federal Student
Aid [FAFSA] form.)
- What desires do you have *now* that you hope will be
fulfilled in college? Answers may include: opportunity to try a new, desired activity; better friendships
based on mutual trust; supportive social networks.

If you know what you're looking for, you're more likely to
find it.

Know that college is not Disney World—a place where
your every wish will be magically fulfilled while you bask in
the sun all day and party all night. (If that's your expectation for college, you're in for a rude awakening!) Yet you can
prepare for college admissions by learning about yourself and
identifying your desires and areas for growth. From there,
work backward: find links between your interests and the resources offered by particular colleges and evaluate your top
choices in the light of where you would grow the most and be
the happiest.

Note: A college's brand name may have *nothing* to do with
your chance for happiness there. And remember—you're "interviewing" colleges just as much as they're interviewing you.
Recognize your own power and your ability to make the best
choice for your future.

A PERSONAL MEDITATION

Repeat this mantra to yourself as an affirmation that you can
accomplish anything:

I am me.

I will reflect on what is right for me.

I will not let well-intentioned guidance dictate what is
*	right for me.*

I will not dwell on my shortcomings and failures.

I will not let others' shortcomings and failures limit me.

I will not let negative thoughts stop me from reaching my
*	goals.*

I can find support in any number of ways.

I am enough.

I can succeed; I am successful.

The better you know yourself, the easier your decisions become. And the more you can believe in yourself, the more you can achieve. Trust yourself and know that you have the ability to choose your own path and pursue it.

For more on how to trust yourself . . . keep reading.

FIVE

Know Your Needs

Know Thyself.

—INSCRIBED ON THE TEMPLE OF APOLLO AT DELPHI

By now I hope you're understanding that your college choice should be made *for* you and *by* you—not to please any of the authority figures in your life. I hope you're learning how to tune in to your inner voice and block out the noises that clutter the airwaves. The sooner you learn how to do this, the better set up for life you'll be. You don't want to be 40 years old, regretting that you haven't yet learned how to live for yourself and don't know what to do for the remainder of your time here on earth.

Honoring your needs will lead you to the college that's the best fit for you. As you come to know yourself better and better, you'll know what you need in order to have a happy life. The more specific you are in naming your needs without apology, the better your chances of finding a school where those needs are met. Think about it: What would you do if you were at a restaurant and ordered a hamburger, yet the server came out with tomato soup on the tray? You were *craving* that hamburger and would get a sinking feeling when the server placed the less-filling substitute in front of you. Would you pick up your spoon and eat the soup, as if everything was just fine?

I hope not! I hope you'd take a stand for what you really want and need—and send the soup back. Think of a restaurant menu as you think about your college options. With all of the choices available to you, what do you *need* from your college experience? Your needs don't have to match up with anyone else's. (Maybe your friend ordered the tomato soup, because that's what she was craving!) Get clear on what's important to *you*; that way, you won't get your priorities mixed up with anyone else's.

For instance: maybe you've got a tight friend group and everyone is planning on going to a state school that's only an hour away. Yet you *know* you need to go away for college. This could be for a number of reasons—you want to experience a different part of the country (or a different country altogether), you're attracted to a particular school's academic program, or your family has a legacy at a certain school that you want to continue. On a less happy note—maybe you're eager to escape a difficult home situation, and the thought of putting thousands of miles between you and your folks is appealing. You're certain of your desire to get away—yet you feel confused when your friends talk about how great life will be when everyone's together at the state school, how much fun it will be to come home every weekend.

In this chapter we'll meet people who were clear on their

own needs and thus able to ignore what they thought they "should" want in a college. You're not going to college for anyone else, and no one else will live your college experience. Putting your needs *first* is not selfish: it's pragmatic.

Melissa Dahl is someone who put her own needs first when it came to choosing a career path and college. She knew her own strengths and played to them, in high school and beyond. Today Melissa is living the career of her dreams, thanks to her ability to know her own needs and honor them.

. . . .

Melissa Dahl: Finding a Career Path and Choosing the Right College

Growing up, Melissa Dahl was *painfully* shy. Melissa was so shy she was uncomfortable interacting with others even in low-risk scenarios, like speaking to the babysitter or giving her order at a restaurant. That kind of shyness can be crippling; it's hard to be so stifled in communication, especially when it seems like everyone around us has no problems talking to people. But one day, Melissa came across an essay written by a journalist: the journalist said that she too had been an extremely shy kid but that her journalism career allowed her the ability to talk to people. The journalist could approach people and ask them questions for her job; her career afforded her an entry point into more unguarded communication with others.

Melissa immediately recognized herself in the story. Maybe *she* could overcome her shyness as a journalist, too!

A career path was set in motion. For her seventh-grade English class, Melissa had to do a presentation on a career she might pursue one day. Melissa picked journalism . . . and she stuck with that choice throughout high school, college, and into adulthood. With her future career as a journalist in mind, Melissa set out to choose a college with a great journalism program.

But academic offerings weren't the only factor in Melissa's decision; she also craved a college experience that didn't involve moving far away from home. Melissa was a kid who didn't really have a hometown. Wisconsin was "home base," but Melissa and her family moved away when she was six. Melissa's father was a consultant for hospitals, and the family frequently moved for his job. When Melissa was in high school, the family was living in California. She felt a need to stay put and checked out various colleges in California.

Melissa found that the University of California schools like UC Berkeley and UCLA were STEM focused and didn't have the type of journalism program she desired. That narrowed her choice to California state universities (CSUs). Melissa ended up choosing Cal State Sacramento for two reasons. Number one: the school had a great journalism program, with many graduates finding jobs at the *Sacramento Bee* after graduation. Number two: the school was "insanely affordable," according to Melissa. She was able to graduate without any debt.

We'll get into student loans and their impact on you and your financial future later in this chapter. But for now, know this: student loans can be a major financial burden that you carry for years—decades, even—*after* college graduation. According to PayScale.com, the average starting salary for a journalist beginning his or her career is $26,000 to $75,000.[1] Let's say Melissa graduated college and got a job that paid on the low end of that scale, or around $30,000 per year. That equals $2,500 a month, before taxes. Now, consider: Melissa would have to pay for housing, health care, food, and other expenses (clothes, Netflix, dinner with friends) out of that paycheck. Now, imagine if she were paying an additional $500 a month in student loans . . . that's financial strain that Melissa was better off without! Not only was Melissa able to select a college that brilliantly prepared her for her future career as a journalist—she did so while honoring her needs to stay rooted near her home in California and to have an affordable college experience.

What matters most is that Melissa *liked* Cal State Sacramento. She felt happy there. Melissa's choice was driven by practicality, her future goals, and a need to feel comfortable at college. What do *you* need from your future college?

Melissa did become a journalist, by the way. She got an internship at the *Sacramento Bee* her junior year and soon had the opportunity to write feature stories. After college, Melissa began work in online journalism at MSNBC. She's currently a senior editor for *New York* magazine's The Cut, and her work has appeared in *Elle, Parents,* and TODAY.com. Melissa's first book, *Cringeworthy: A Theory of Awkwardness,* was published in 2018.

LESSONS FROM MELISSA'S STORY

The things you view as weaknesses could turn out to be your greatest strengths.

• Are there certain parts of your personality that you believe are holding you back? For instance: do you have a tendency to speak "too much" . . . or too little? Do you often think, "If I could just change *this* part of my personality, then life would be easier"?

• If so, consider flipping that thought on its head. How could you work *with* that part of your personality? For Melissa, her natural introversion became an asset in her career as a journalist; she could hone in on the other person, listen intently, and craft a compelling narrative based on what she learned. That's harder to do if you're an extrovert and love talking all the time! If Melissa had been a big talker, a more natural career fit might have been as a politician or salesperson.

• There's not *one* right way to be in the world. Whatever your personality and strengths, there are many different paths to success. Your task is to determine how you can honor your needs, play to your strengths, and craft a career and life that bring you energy rather deplete you.

Evaluate your future college based on the career you want.

• Melissa saw the opportunity to begin her desired career path while in college. She got invaluable experience beyond the classroom by working at the *Sacramento Bee* (and she got paid, too!). Does the college you're considering give you this kind of opportunity? Say you, too, want to be a journalist. Working at the college newspaper is great—but getting outside the "bubble" of college and gaining real-world experience could be even more valuable. If you've got definite ideas about your future career, narrow your choice based on which universities offer chances to practice job skills with professionals.

Think long-term and consider the financial cost of college.
• If you're not lucky enough to have your college bill footed by someone else, seriously consider how much debt (in the form of student loans) you're willing to take on. Evaluate this in terms of your future career. If you're planning to enter a high-income profession, more debt for your degree might make sense. If you're drawn to a career that's not as lucrative (say, social work, education, or journalism), it doesn't make sense to amass six figures in debt. Melissa graduated with zero debt—she even got paid to practice her future career while in college. That's what I call being smart! It's not too early to begin to think about your financial future, even if you've never considered these questions before. Don't let your eyes glaze over in financial aid discussions; pay attention and ask questions. You want

to make the best choices for you *now* and you *ten years from now.*

There's no such thing as a "best" college—there's only a best college for you.

- Don't get tricked into thinking that the only colleges worth applying to are the most selective name-brand schools in the country. Consider this: Sacramento State has an acceptance rate of 68 percent.[2] Considering that Ivy League universities typically have admissions rates of less than 10 percent, some might look at that data and determine that the Ivy League universities are automatically "better" choices. But *there is no such thing as a "best" college!* College admissions is not sports. You don't "win" college admissions like you win a track meet.

- Choosing the best college for you is about *match-making*, not competition. It's about finding the one that's the best match for you. How do you determine this? Like Melissa did: by considering your needs and figuring out which college meets them the best. Your needs are not the same as anyone else's, so it does no good to borrow the criteria your friend is using to make their college choice! Even knowing how your friend came up with their criteria in the first place would require you to be able to peek inside their brain (as well as their mom and dad's bank account). You only know *you* and your situation. Keep your eyes on your own paper as you work out which school is your best match.

Want to learn about another leader who put his needs first and wound up with a great college experience? Read on.

. . . .

Ike Umunnah: A Nurturing Environment That Paved the Way for Future Success

Today, Ike Umunnah is a leader whose experience has been honed across Fortune 500 companies, the military, and in government. Today, he works within the Biden administration, where he is in charge of public affairs for the Economic Development Administration. Ike has his law degree from the University of North Dakota, and his master's in policy and management from the Harvard Graduate School of Education. But before all his success, Ike was a kid living with his single mom, making average grades, and working extra hard to accommodate his learning difference.

For undergraduate, Ike chose Morehouse College. When he visited Morehouse, Ike got the sense that there he would be part of a supportive and nurturing community. The director of admissions met with Ike and his mother for two hours, explaining the ins and outs of the application process and how Ike could succeed in college with his learning disability. Ike was impressed that Morehouse staff took such care to welcome him, even before he'd decided to attend. Says Ike: "By the time fall [of freshman year] came, I knew the registration lady, cafeteria lady, and admissions lady." Ike felt that he had stepped into a new family; he knew that the adults on campus loved and supported him. For a young gay Black man, this environment provided a safe space in which Ike could flourish.

The nurturing and caring community at Morehouse helped Ike through a rough time. During the spring of his junior year, Ike's mother had a stroke, and Ike left school. When it was time for Ike to go back to Morehouse, he couldn't afford it. Luckily, thanks to the advocacy of Morehouse administrators, Ike received a scholarship that allowed him to go back to Morehouse and finish his undergraduate degree.

Had Ike not felt so comfortable within the Morehouse community, he might have viewed his mother's stroke as the end of the line for his college career. Yet those connections he had made—even before he decided on Morehouse as his college choice—proved strong. Ike fostered relationships throughout his undergraduate years and has later benefited from those relationships in his business. Ike has leaned on the strong alumni network at Morehouse as he's navigated his career; in fact, his first business partner was a Morehouse alumnus. Ike quoted his former college dean: "If all you did was come here for the finance courses and are not building relationships, you're wasting your money." Ike said the real value in college is the people you meet: "smart, ambitious, like-minded people to have as part of your network."

Ike immediately felt at home at Morehouse, an HBCU (historically Black college and university), likely much more than he would have felt at a PWI (predominantly white institution). If you're a member of a minority group, how important is it to engage in a supportive, caring community made up

of people who look like you? For many people—like Ike—
choosing such a college can feel like coming home. This type
of college experience can provide a unique opportunity for
deeper self-knowing.

From Ike's college application, to undergrad, to grad
school, and into his career, relationships are what have meant
the most. What are your relationship needs? Which college
would have the greatest chance of fulfilling those needs?

LESSONS FROM IKE'S STORY

Connection is everything.

• Are you drawn to a particular school because the
people in that college community are invested in you?
Your chances of getting into your dream college grow
when you make connections with the people at that
college (more on that in chapter seven!). But building
relationships with faculty and staff is about so much
more than getting in—building these relationships is
a practice that will help you get the most value out
of college and your future career. Many students find
they get more personalized support at smaller liberal
arts colleges rather than big universities; an HBCU
or school where your ethnic group is strongly represented may also be a place to form deep relationships
with people who get you. If you're already building
those relationships, do you feel *connected* to the people
at your school of choice—like they actually care about
you?

If you have learning differences, know how you will be supported in college.

• If, like Ike, you've got a learning disability that can make completing coursework difficult, you may want to choose a school where there is significant support for students like you. Know that you're not alone: one in five students in the United States has a learning disability.[3] If you've received support in high school, you may benefit from support in college, too. At any rate, you'll be required to be much more self-directed in college. That means if you need help, it's up to you to ask for it. Likewise, perhaps your learning style is not a "disability" but is a bit unconventional. If this applies to you, consider going to a school that helps kids who learn differently, like American University in Washington, D.C., Northeastern University in Boston, or Landmark College in Vermont. For a list of colleges that have special supports in place for students with learning disabilities check out guides like Princeton Review's *K & W Guide to Colleges for Students with Learning Differences*.

Life happens, even when you're in college.

• Ike certainly didn't plan on his mom having a stroke his sophomore year. Life happens in the "outside" world, even when you're in college—sicknesses, family moves, financial difficulties, etc. You may experience your own difficulties as a college student, too. Know that if you get sick or have a family emergency, it's not the end of the world. It's okay to take care of yourself and do what you need to do for your family, even if that means leaving college for a semester or two.

Had Ike not invested so much in his relationships at Morehouse, coming back may have been an even harder choice. If something happens when you're at college, who will you turn to? Have this question in mind from freshman orientation onward—not to be morbid or pessimistic, but so you'll remember the value of making connections with faculty who care about you. Make it a point to be known by name by professors and college staff whom you admire. Don't be intimidated by the years and degrees that separate you and a caring professor; take the chance and build a relationship. You'll gain so much more from your college experience if you do.

Student Loan Debt—How Much Is Too Much?

According to credit.com, students graduating in 2019 had an average of $31,172 in student loan debt per person. This translates to a monthly payment of $393, with graduates taking 10–30 years to pay off their debt. Thirty thousand may sound like a high number... but I've known people with much, much larger tabs from their undergraduate and graduate degrees. Think six figures and *multiple* six figures.

Now factor in the cost of interest. Let's say you graduate with $50,000 in debt from a loan at 10 percent interest. (That's a really high interest rate, but we'll use it for the purpose of illustration.) If you want to pay the loan in ten years, your monthly payment will be $660.75. What you actually pay for that loan is

$79,290.44—almost $30,000 *more* than the original amount of the loan. That $29,290.44 is your interest payment. Yikes!

Student loan debt becomes a burden you carry into adulthood. What happens if you meet someone you want to marry or be with long-term . . . yet your partner *also* has a huge amount of student debt? How will the two of you stick together, make a plan for paying off the debt, and do the other things you may want to do, like buy a house or have children?

These are "adult" questions that may be millions of miles from your mind right now. I get it. But even if you've never thought about money in this way, managing your money is a huge part of adult life. If you're not lucky enough to have your college bill entirely footed, either by relatives or your university of choice, you need to think long-term about the amount of debt you're willing to take on and at least *begin* thinking about how you'll pay it off.

How much debt is too much? There's no way anyone can answer that question for you. But as I mentioned earlier in this chapter: consider the career you want to enter. Is it one with high earning potential? If so, taking on more debt may make sense. But keep in mind: *you may change your mind*. People switch majors all the time, or they go to grad school for something completely different than what they studied in undergrad. Let's say you have a sucky experience at your first college of choice, which also happens to be very expensive. You switch to a local state school, where you're much happier and the price tag is lower. You'll still be paying off your crummy year for a long time to come . . . which can leave a sour taste in your mouth.

How to Not Be Clueless About How Your College Is Being Paid For

Luckily, a little financial self-knowledge will go a long way toward your financial peace of mind. You don't have to be stuck with a six-figure student loan bill. You could even graduate from college debt-free! (Plenty of people do it . . . why not you?) Take the blinders off and know what kind of money future you're signing up for when you give your acceptance to a school.

Be active in financial aid discussions with whoever is helping you in the college application process.

Think financial aid is a topic for Mom and Dad only? Think again! First off, fill out the FAFSA (Free Application for Federal Student Aid). According to the National Center for Education Statistics, about 25 percent of high school students don't complete it.[4] Nearly a quarter don't complete a *free* form . . . for *free money.* Don't make that mistake! Don't forget the CSS Profile, too, which is required for some colleges to provide you with need- and merit-based financial aid.[5] After you've filled out the FAFSA, pay extra close attention in college financial discussions. Don't let your eyes glaze over and don't let prospective universities get away with lazy answers to your questions. What loan package are they recommending to you? What's the interest rate for each loan? Typical repayment times? Shop around; if you're choosing between several colleges, which has the best aid package? If you've got your heart set on one school that is offering a smaller amount of financial aid, while your second choice is giving you more help, could you use the second school's offer as leverage against the first? (Say, "Hey, school XYZ is offering me *this* . . . could you all match that or do better?")

Get savvy. Advocate for yourself at every turn. Don't hit snooze at the expense of your future financial security.

Now, I'm sorry to tell my friends who need to complete the FAFSA that you can actually get an admissions advantage if you don't request financial aid. Why? Because colleges are looking for students who can afford to pay full tuition, which helps colleges to fund the tuition for students who can't. It's a classic "robbing Peter to pay Paul" situation, but such is the truth and you should know it.

If no one's guiding you toward smart financial decisions, seek out that guidance for yourself.

Let's say your primary caregiver *isn't* helping you navigate the finances of college. That's not an ideal situation—yet if you find yourself in it, you're not alone. Ask yourself: Who else could help me figure this out?

Maybe you have a financially savvy aunt you could turn to for advice, or a mentor figure at your house of worship. You could seek advice from a trusted guidance counselor or former teacher. Leave no stone unturned; if you remember something someone random told you about paying for college—even if it was years ago—look up that person and ask for the help you need.

Look for resources online.

It's super important that you follow tip number two and talk to a trusted adult who can give you sound financial advice on college. Don't skip that step. But luckily, you're not solely dependent on in-person help; we live in the information age, where a world of resources is at your fingertips! There are countless websites devoted to highlighting scholarships for which you might be eligible. Go to studentaid .gov to fill out the FAFSA. At the time of writing, the FAFSA application opens on October 1 of each year. Fill out the FAFSA as close to the opening date as possible to maximize your chances for aid. In addition, check out scholarships. For example, scholarships.com allows you to search 3.7 *million* college scholarships and grants. Of course, go to your top choice's college website to learn more about specific scholarships and aid packages available to the student body.

If you're freaked about the money side of college, take a deep breath. Don't be scared; get curious instead. What financial aid is out there for you? How can you get creative? What resources exist—perhaps unknown to you right now— that could change everything? Explore, explore, and then explore some more.

(Just be sure you fill out that FAFSA and CSS Profile if you need it, okay?)

Exercise: What Do You Need From College?

Melissa needed a local college that was affordable and would set her up well for her future career as a journalist. Ike needed a supportive environment where he felt the faculty truly cared for him, and where he could be his full self.

What do you need from college?

Below is a list of needs your future college *could* meet for you. Beside each item, rank it on a scale of 1 to 4. 1 = non-negotiable, 2 = important, 3 = semi-important, 4 = unimportant.

- Long distance from current home
- Friends from high school will be there
- Internship opportunities in my future career
- Politically engaged student body
- Near nature, lots of outdoor activities
- Affordable
- Attractive program in my desired major
- School with high name-brand recognition, prestigious
- Good sorority/fraternity scene
- Beautiful environment
- Cool college town, lots of off-campus opportunities
- Strong study abroad program
- Strong religious affiliation/spiritual opportunities
- Strong alumni network
- Chance to play collegiate sports
- Diverse student body
- Can drive home easily

This list is by no means comprehensive. You may have a completely different set of priorities than the ones listed here.

The point is this: the sooner you get real about what your needs are, the sooner you can cross schools from your list that don't meet them. You're the one going to college; you're the boss of your experience.

SIX

Trust Your Gut

Never apologize for trusting your intuition.
Your brain can play tricks, your heart can be blind,
but your gut is always right.

—RACHEL WOLCHIN

I know you're in high school and thinking about college—you're preparing for the rest of your life, and you've got a lot of it left to live. Yet I want you to think ahead to the very *end* of your life. (A bit morbid, but stay with me.) Who do you hope to *be* at that point? What do you hope you'll have done? How can you live *now*, at the beginning of your life, so that you won't have regrets at the end?

Two of the things people express the most regret for at the end of their lives are 1) not having trusted themselves enough, and 2) having cared too much about what other people thought. These two regrets are opposite sides of the same coin. If we don't trust *ourselves*, we look to everyone around us to tell us who we are and what we should do. We then live our lives playing by someone else's rulebook. If we're living for someone else—either consciously or unconsciously—we'll never be "good" enough! If you let the people around you dictate the terms of your life, believe me, they will. And the people around you will always show you the ways you're not measuring up or how you could be doing more.

That's no way to live. (Clearly—if it were, the dying wouldn't say how much they regretted this lifestyle.) By contrast, when you trust yourself, you learn to believe that *you are enough*, just as you are. You begin to see that there is not anything you can *do* that will make you worthy of love and happiness. You don't need to have a GPA over 4.0, or get into the Ivy League, or be captain of your swim team, or host a record-breaking fundraiser. Trusting yourself is less about doing and more about getting still—still enough to hear, recognize, and honor your own voice. When you're being true to yourself, the opinions of others become less and less important. As the quote that begins this chapter states, your gut always knows the right way forward. Your brain may play games by trying to convince you of what you *should* want; your heart can get confused, trying to please everyone around you. But your gut won't steer you wrong.

Once you learn how to trust your gut, you can live your best life without regrets. The people you'll meet in this chapter trusted their own inner guidance systems over the well-intentioned advice of authority figures. These role models took actions that may not have made sense to anyone else. Yet they knew that, ultimately, they'd only have themselves to answer to. The sooner you come to this awareness, the freer you are to live your own life.

. . . .

Jorge Torres: A College Choice for an Inclusive Community

Jorge Torres was a first-generation college student in his family and had to complete the application process entirely on his own. Back when Jorge applied in the early 1990s, his family didn't own a computer, so he dictated his college applications while his father typed them up on the family typewriter. Amid his dad's cigarette smoke and a steady soundtrack of U2, Jorge and his family got the applications completed.

Jorge's hard work paid off; he was accepted to several of his top-choice colleges. Jorge ultimately selected Yale, because it seemed like such a positive place for people of color.

"The Ivies were on my radar because I was just a really ambitious, motivated, high-achieving high school student," said Jorge. While a lot of college applicants drool over *any* Ivy, the Ivy League brand was less important to Jorge than finding a place where he could be truly himself. Jorge learned that, for him, not every Ivy was created equal. He got a not-so-great feeling about Princeton; Jorge didn't like that students of color gathered in a place they called the "Third World Center." He was appalled that a name like that would exist in the early nineties.

At Yale, though, Jorge picked up on a different vibe.

"What my choice came down to was the feeling that I had with the communities of color at Yale," said Jorge. "There was a much richer campus life around cultural groups [than other colleges I visited] that involved political stuff, cultural stuff, and service. New Haven was a big factor [in my decision] because it was a real city, and so Yale just seemed to have a richer experience for me."

This "it" factor Jorge felt is not something you can find in a brochure or through browsing online. Jorge had to scope out the schools for himself and trust his gut on where he belonged.

Trusting his gut instinct is a skill that has served Jorge well, throughout college and long past his graduation. As Jorge progressed in his career, he didn't confine himself to just one path and has made many changes along the way. Jorge is a lawyer, entrepreneur, venture capitalist, *and* a professor—that's a lot of credentials on a resume! Yet each role has led naturally to the next as Jorge continues to be guided by an inner sense of what he wants and doesn't want. Trusting in this sense has allowed Jorge's career to unfold so brilliantly.

For Jorge, professional freedom is what it's all about. "I am drawn to opportunities where I have the space to define the terms on which I'm going to do business and who I'm going to work with," he said. Jorge recognizes that opportunities are always available, and that making one choice does not close him off to a host of other possibilities. (Remember the quote attributed to George Eliot: "It is never too late to be what you might have been.") Whatever situation Jorge creates for himself, he is able to trust his gut and determine the right next step.

What lessons can you learn from Jorge?

- **The right college is not always about just the academics.** Whether or not a college offers the courses you need for your future career is important, but there are so many other factors to consider—the student population and whether or not you feel comfortable with this group, school culture, the actual location of the university, the surrounding community, and the opportunities provided off-campus . . . just to name a few. College presents you with endless options. You could stay half an hour from Mom and Dad or branch out and go somewhere across the country; you could go with a bestie or make a completely new identity for yourself. What do you want from these four years? Don't let the lure of a brand-name school keep you from looking at whether or not it will enrich your *whole* self—not just your resume.

- **Culture fit matters.** At Yale, Jorge experienced a welcoming environment and could easily envision himself participating in the activities available there. Before you select a college, make sure you—at the very least—talk with people who have attended or who are attending the college. Try to take a visit to the college and explore the resources available to students; get a feel for which resources might be a fit for you. This will give you a good idea about how much you will enjoy the campus experience.

- **Don't choose a college that you don't have a good feeling about.** Had Jorge gone to a different college, like Princeton, he might have felt that he made the wrong choice even if others told him it was "better" than Yale. A gut feeling is a good enough reason to say *no* to any college (even an Ivy!). Also, when you're looking for colleges, think about whether you want to be in a city, suburb, or rural area. You could even look into going to college abroad. The bottom line: this is *your* experience, not anyone else's. Don't go to a college that just doesn't feel like you.

Love the idea of being a multi-hyphenate professor-entrepreneur? Check out another incredible story from Wharton professor and marketing legend Peter Fader at www.getrealandgetin.com.

. . . .

Client Story: When Trusting Your Gut Means Taking a Big Risk

Just like Jorge, my student June has a knack for trusting her gut. June is currently embarking on an adventurous World Bachelor in Business program at USC, an elite global academic business program affiliated with USC, Bocconi University in Milan, and Hong Kong University of Science and Technology. June wants to be a global entrepreneur one day, so she chose a fitting global experience for college.

But this opportunity never would have existed if June hadn't trusted her gut from a very young age—ninth grade, to be exact. When June was a 14-year-old middle school student in India, she was unsatisfied by her educational experience. Rather than be confined to studies that were heavily science and math focused, June wanted a chance to explore her interest in business and world cultures. June begged her parents to let her go to high school in the United States—all by herself.

June's parents were able to send her to a prestigious private school in Connecticut. Once June got to Connecticut, she flourished. June carried a 4.19 GPA with a challenging course load and scored well on her SAT.

But more important than her excellent academic performance were the experiences June created for herself in high school. June was able to pursue her interests in business and entrepreneurship by founding a business and entrepreneurship club. This club required her to learn and utilize skills in website design, fundraising, and organizational leadership. June also participated in a prestigious summer business program, where she honed her skills in business planning and presentation. Through her participation in these endeavors, June acquired important entrepreneurial skills such as financial management, sponsorship, and peer leadership.

In addition, June served as president of the South Asian culture club at her high school and as treasurer for the student government. She participated on the dance team and served as a prefect in the school's dormitory. June also dedicated many hours to volunteer work. Her involvement in these organizations allowed June to learn about diplomacy and collaboration.

June was a positive force for her high school's community spirit. She was entrusted with many leadership roles and responsibilities. These opportunities positioned her to compete for admission against students with higher grades and standardized test results.

To gain entrance to USC, June needed guidance on constructing a powerful essay and resume that would highlight her experiences and accomplishments *outside* of her academics.

Through her dedication to her pursuits and strong sense of personal discipline, June was able to create a portfolio that made her stand out in the application process. While she was rejected from several colleges, June was admitted into the *exact right* program for her: the USC World Bachelor in Business. We can learn a lot from June's example.

LESSONS FROM JUNE'S STORY

- **If you want to get admissions officers to pay attention** to you, don't tell them about all the wonderful things you *will* do in the future once they let you into their school: show them all the ways you are making an impact *now*. After all, if you aren't making any impact in your communities *now*, why should they believe you will do so once you have graduated? Admissions officers want to see the evidence of your impact *where you already are*. So show them. Trust your gut as you create experiences that will increase your visibility and impact. Then your application can't help but stand out.

- **Advocate for yourself to get the opportunities you want.** Had June sat back and hoped for the best for her future, she would still be in India and not in a position to get admitted to USC. She would not have access to the resources she has now in her quest to become a global entrepreneur. June pitched her educational goals to her parents, and later to admissions officers, which earned her the best possible opportunities. Even if your family doesn't have the means to support you as June's family did, seek out the people who *can* help. They're out there.

- **Don't dwell on your shortcomings.** June's SAT score, though good, was not as strong as she would have liked.* She endured plenty of rejections from colleges before getting that letter from USC. But everything worked out brilliantly—this program is practically tailor-made for June! Even if your path to college looks different than you thought it would, don't give up. Rejection is going to be a part of your life as you apply for college, during college, and after graduation. Keep knocking on doors and turning over stones until you find a route that's perfectly suited to you.

REFLECTION QUESTIONS

Trusting your gut isn't just a practice that will help you navigate your college choice and future career—it's a practice that will help you steer away from potentially harmful people and situations. Your gut wants to keep you safe. Think about it: we are mammals, with animal instincts. The more you learn to trust your instincts, the safer you will be—like the deer who hears the snap of a twig in the woods and knows to run before the hunter can spot her.

Have you ever had a gut feeling that a certain person wasn't safe to be around? Have you turned to a friend at a party

---

* If you're an international student, your scores need to be in the top 75 percent of published ranges for elite universities in order for you to have the best shot at admission.

because you *just knew* it was time to go? Have you seen someone creepy walking down the street and known that it was time to steer to the other side and find other people, pronto?

That is your gut speaking to you. These examples are not meant to scare you; rather, I want you to connect with what it *feels* like to trust your instincts and to follow them. Chances are, you've done it before. When you get a message from your gut, the key is not to think too hard (or at all, depending on the situation), to receive a signal from the animal part of yourself and to *act* on it. It's all right if the message doesn't make sense to your logical brain.

You can trust your gut feelings. If your parents hype up a certain university but every time you think of going there you get a sinking feeling—*that's a sign*. If, like Jorge, you get a bad taste in your mouth from a certain university—*that's a sign*. It's in your best interest to hone your gut instinct now and to learn how to listen to it. Remember: in college, you're going to be the one primarily responsible for your safety and well-being. You may be used to talking things to death with Mom and Dad, or getting input from 30 different people before making a decision, but you may not have that luxury in college (especially if you're in a situation where your safety is on the line).

You're going to be surrounded by thousands of people with whom you have no history. You can't rely on your friends or authority figures to tell you who's shady and who's legit: you'll have to ask those questions of yourself and rely on your own internal guidance system. Below are reflection questions meant to put you in touch with your own instincts. Write your answers to these questions; study them; know yourself. Your gut instinct is there to protect you and steer you toward the life of your dreams, so get familiar *now* with how this instinct speaks to you.

1. What does it *feel* like to trust your gut? (What does it *literally* feel like, in your body? Are there certain cues your body gives you to tell you that something's important?)
2. How do you know something is or isn't right for you? Write about the way your body responds to a thought, idea, or person that you know *is* right for you. Now, what about something that *isn't*? Write about what that feels like, too.
3. Have you ever gone against your gut? Write about the situation. What happened after?
4. Now, what did you learn from the situation? What could you do differently next time?

What practices do you currently have in your life that clear out the noise in your head and allow you to hear what your gut is telling you? Physical activity, like running, yoga, or dance, can powerfully connect you with your body and gut instinct. Meditation is another great tool to help you tune out the noise and listen to your innermost wisdom.

Whatever your practice, I encourage you to continue doing it when you get to college. (Or find something else you love and do that instead.) A physical activity and mindfulness habit will help you reduce stress in college; it will also provide you with a continual connection to the part of you that isn't influenced by the world's projections or your own anxieties. Exercise and meditation connect you with your wild, wise, animal self—your gut self. It will tell you everything you need to know.

SEVEN

It's Who You Know (and Who Knows You)

It's not who you know, it's who knows you.

—ANONYMOUS

In the business world, there's a quote that's so widely used it's almost trite: "It's not *what* you know, it's *who* you know." Connecting with the most exciting opportunities and landing your dream job is less about your know-how and more about your network. Have you ever heard of "six degrees of separation"? This purports that each individual on Earth is removed from every *other* individual by only six people (or less). Taking this principle to heart, you're only six people away from Taylor Swift, Bill Gates, and Beyoncé. When I was young we'd play the "Kevin Bacon Game," which is based on this principle of six degrees of separation. In this game, you think of a movie or actor, link it back to another movie or actor, and eventually get back to Kevin Bacon within six people.

As I mentioned in the introductory chapter, my celebrity idols were the kids in the band Hanson (I've moved up in the world since then!). At the time Hanson rose to popularity in 1997, my father worked for a food service trade publication whose parent company was the same as *Billboard Magazine*'s. Even though my dad did not have a connection to Hanson, *Billboard* did. My dad made a cold call to someone; I nervously took the phone and expressed my Hanson love. Lo and behold: I wound up with highly sought after (free!) tickets to an on-camera taped performance at New York City's Beacon Theatre. This performance later appeared on Hanson's highly popular VHS (ever heard of those?) *Tulsa, Tokyo & the Middle of Nowhere*.

Was I connected to Hanson? Not really, but my family and I got creative in thinking about our connections. Because we thought outside the box, I was able to see my celebrity idols at a very special concert that I still remember fondly. In fact, attending this concert was one of the experiences that inspired me to enter the music business.

But my family and I didn't just go to the Hanson concert, take photos, scream, and forget our *Billboard Magazine* connection. We followed up with a personal thank-you note and a box of chocolates. We showed our contact that she'd done so much more than just give us "free stuff"; our *Billboard* connection gave us a treasured family memory. Who knew that taking the time to say a special thank-you would result in extra, invite-only Hanson concerts the following year?

This was a fabulous bonus but *not* something we expected when we sent the chocolates. Building relationships isn't transactional. You don't just use people and let them go; you have to express appreciation for those who go out of their way to help you. Thanks to my parents, our *Billboard* connection, and Hanson, I learned this lesson early.

But let's say you weren't born into a wealthy family with well-connected parents or a father like mine who's willing to make phone calls for you. You may see your peers' parents arranging meetings, interviews, and internships for them; your friend says they want something, Mom and Dad pull a few strings, and voilà! Your talentless friend is now in an extremely hard-to-get-into summer camp for musical theater. For your well-connected friend, the game is stacked in terms of college admissions (or a meeting with Hanson).

Rest assured: "it's who you know" is not all about rich parents schmoozing with college presidents at cocktail parties. Not by a long shot. Whether or not you consider yourself well connected, you *can* form and nurture relationships with key individuals at your college of choice and thereby better your chances of getting into your dream school. You're not dependent on your parents or any other adults in your life. And it's relatively easy for you, given your access to email and social media, to connect with *anyone* in the world; most people's email addresses are listed online, and you can find company emails on hunter.io. It's *your* responsibility (and pleasure!) to connect with people who can help you post–high school.

Colleges—unlike the kind woman at *Billboard*—care about *your* leadership, not your parents' connections. One way to show leadership is to get out there and make the connection yourself. If you're used to securing opportunities via your parents, this suggestion may come as a jolt. If your parents are clueless about college admissions—whether due to neglect, ignorance of the process, the busy-ness of life and working multiple jobs, or any other reason—this is *good* news. In either scenario, the key factor is *you*: how well you can form relationships, provide value, and ask for help from those further along the path than you.

Consider also the quote at the top of this chapter: "It's not who you know, it's who knows you." The *number* of relationships you have with "important" individuals (that's sarcasm—every person is important) at your school of choice is meaningless. How many of those people know *you*? Think of all the contacts in your phone—they probably number in the hundreds or even thousands. Yet how many do you text on a regular basis? How many text you?

Strong, healthy relationships require give and take. That means it's not enough for you, the applicant, to bombard representatives of your chosen university with email after email, desperately hoping for a leg up in admissions. "It's not who you know, it's who knows you" is about forming genuine connections with individuals at colleges you're considering. If talking to adults and forming connections isn't something you're doing right now—if you're clueless about how to even start—don't worry. Non-slimy networking is a skill that can be learned. We'll cover the basics in this chapter; I'll even give you email scripts you can adapt as needed.

At the beginning of this book, I told you about my obsession with NYU. By sophomore year of high school, I'd decided that NYU was *the* school for me, and I made it my mission to be known by the admissions reps. I went to every single open house and information session that the school offered. Was that the best use of my time and energy? Probably not—but it didn't hurt, either. At least I was known!

Looking back, I can see that I was overzealous. I didn't need to do *everything* I did to get into NYU—but there were a few key activities that helped me become known by the people at the school. (Remember: no matter how much you build up a school in your mind, it's made up of people just like you and me.) Most likely, I could have focused only on these three things and left all the rest.

First, I attended the departmental open house for Steinhardt. This is the NYU school that offered the music business degree I so badly wanted. Second, I went to a regional open house near my home in New Jersey and met face-to-face with an admissions director. Third, I spent a day with a professor in my chosen program, a person who would later become a favorite teacher and mentor.

Okay; for the third one, I had help. Professor Walter Reinhold had been my father's professor as well; my dad re-connected with him and arranged the meeting. My dad, Professor Reinhold, and I spent a lovely day together. Because he was impressed with me, Professor Reinhold wrote me a stellar email recommendation to admissions. I benefited big time from my dad's connection . . . but this never would have "worked" if I hadn't already been 100 percent *sold* on NYU. I was determined to put my best foot forward in that meeting. My dedication and interest were palpable. There was no place on earth I would have rather been than in Professor Reinhold's home; I hung on his every word and treasured our day together.

When parents arrange meetings and you're an unwilling or semi-willing bystander, "It's who you know" falls flat. I see it all too often; a parent will set up a meeting with a college rep, saying, "You just *have* to meet Johnny, he's so interested in XYZ!" As it turns out, Johnny has *zero* interest in the thing his parents have been hyping. If you're not inherently interested in a college or major—if your *parents* are actually the ones with the interest—it shows, and it's not a good look for you. Meeting key reps from your *parents'* favorite college is a waste of everyone's time.

That's why we've spent so much time in this book working to identify what it is *you* want. Connecting with individuals at your top-choice school is a bold move. You need the courage of your convictions, and you need to make sure it's your dream—not someone else's. But forming relationships with reps of your chosen school is *so* worthwhile, and when you learn how to do it right, it's not that scary.

In this chapter, we'll study some people who went all in on forming relationships with mentors: before college, during college, and beyond. Forming connections, adding value to others, and asking for help when you need it is an art; below I tell stories of people who have mastered it. You can do this, too.

. . . .

Illana Raia: A Tradition of Mentorship

Illana Raia, founder and CEO of Être and author of *Être: Girls, Who Do You Want to Be?*, always knew she wanted to be a lawyer. She'd grown up around the law and seen her grandmother's career as an attorney. Illana also knew she was interested in attending a women's college; her mother, aunt, and other family members had attended women's colleges and spoke highly of the experience. Armed with this information about her interests and preferences, Illana visited Smith College—a women's college in Northampton, Massachusetts—in search of the perfect college fit.

Right away, Illana felt at home. She was impressed by the young women on Smith's campus, who had big ideas and were doing big things. Illana loved listening to these young women, who put no limits on what they were capable of. The Smith students' energy and ambition drew her to the school, where she ultimately attended. For Illana, finding the right college was key to her future success. To this day she says of her time in college: "I truly think I'd be fundamentally different if I hadn't gone to Smith."

Illana dove right into studying law at Smith and later at the University of Chicago. She couldn't get enough of her political theory and constitutional law classes. But what Illana appreciated most were the fantastic mentors surrounding her. Illana got the chance to study under legendary figures in American law; not only that, but she got to study *them*. When Illana graduated from law school and began her career as a corporate lawyer, she was paired with a mentor whom she describes as "the most inspirational woman you'll ever meet."

Fast forward a few years: Illana transitioned out of the workplace upon having children and then back into it when her youngest started kindergarten six years later.

When she entered the workforce for a second time, Illana had a new role: building internal websites for her former firm.

Prior to landing the job, Illana had *zero* tech experience. But Illana had built good relationships in her workplace before the birth of her daughter. When she felt it was time to go back to work, she leaned on these relationships; Illana's peers helped her carve out a new role that was better suited to her life as a mom with young kids.

Fast forward again: Illana's daughter was in middle school. Illana wanted to draw together all of the amazing women in her network to give her daughter advice before she launched into the world. Illana had the idea for a summit in her home; she would gather her friends—writers, surgeons, news anchors, CEOs, etc.—to share what they had learned through decades in the workforce. Due to the difficulty of coordinating everyone's schedules, the summit never happened. But what *did* happen was something even better.

Of her planned summit, Illana's friends told her: "You're not thinking big enough." Illana had gained deep tech experience through building all of the sites for her law firm. Her friends posed the idea: Why not create an online forum where girls could gain advice from the types of powerful women Illana had hoped to gather in her home? Illana took that idea and ran with it: Être was born. The website etregirls.com asks middle school girls the question: What do you want to be? The site connects them to accomplished women doing cool things in the world; young girls can look to older role models—just as Illana did in her youth and adulthood—and model themselves on the best.

LESSONS FROM ILLANA'S STORY

It pays to have an attitude of gratitude.

• Listening to Illana, you'd think she never had a bad teacher or boss. To hear her tell it, she was extremely lucky to be surrounded by great minds when she visited Smith, studied in undergrad and grad school, and then launched in her career. Lucky for her . . . she got all the good mentors and role models! But the rest of us can't count on being surrounded by such stellar examples—right?

• Wrong. I'm *sure* it wasn't all sunshine and roses for Illana at every part of her journey—nobody has a perfect path. But Illana has something that allows her to make the most of any situation and seize opportunities wherever they crop up: an attitude of gratitude. Why did Illana see the best in her mentors and talk about how much her life was transformed through knowing them? Because at each point in her journey, Illana was grateful for where she was while recognizing that there was so much more she could learn. Who in your life right now is a mentor to you? Have you leaned into that connection as hard as you can—not to get something in the *future*, but to learn all you can and be the best you can be *right now*? Illana wasn't using people to get ahead; she was grateful for where she was and went all in, whether that was in college or work. As a result, doors opened for her when she needed them to.

• Also, don't depend on finding your *one* perfect mentor. Rather, think of forming a tribe of mentors, as Illana did at each stage in her journey. One person will not be your fount of wisdom—but you probably have many people surrounding you who could make your way a little smoother. For instance: one person may be a finance whiz who can help you with scholarship and loan applications. Another mentor may be a creative thinker who sees possibilities you couldn't have imagined. Recognize that everyone knows something you don't know; you can have many teachers and mentors as you reach for your dreams. All you have to do is ask.

To work with the best, you have to be the best.
• Illana didn't get amazing opportunities by schmoozing. She worked hard and added value wherever she was. Hard work is what allowed her to sit in the room with top minds in grad school and as a corporate lawyer. Smooth talk will only get you so far. You want to make connections with leaders at your top-choice college or in your field? Show up, be kind, and do the work. What you *do* speaks volumes louder than anything you say.

Don't think of making connections; think of making friends.
• Illana had a six-year work gap when she was at home raising her children. But she'd made strong connections at her law firm, and when it was time to re-enter the

workforce, Illana called on those connections. Working with her peers, Illana crafted a new role for herself.

• When my dad set up the meeting with Professor Reinhold, he'd been out of college for *decades*. Yet Professor Reinhold was still willing to give up an entire day to spend with my dad and me. Making connections is about so much more than meeting people in order to get something (namely, entrance into your top-choice college) in the short term. It's about getting to know *people* and building genuine relationships with them. Remember that each person you connect with is a three-dimensional human being. Be a real person every place you show up; recognize that everyone around you—even the "gate-keepers" of your school of choice—are real people, too.

Do you fashion yourself as a trailblazing, female entrepreneur or think you might become one someday? Visit getrealandgetin.com to read about the incredible journey of fashion designer Elaine Turner.

. . . .

Client Stories: Lana and Neil

Whether or not you consider yourself a networking pro, you can learn the skills needed to build relationships with key people at your college of choice. These skills will be useful to you now and forevermore. Take a cue from Lana and Neil, two students I helped gain acceptance into their dream colleges.

Lana had the dream of attending Princeton but was not a legacy and lacked connections on campus. Lana visited the campus, traveling the long distance with her mother from their native Canada. During her campus visit Lana took two courses, and her mother used the "six degrees of separation" principle to connect Lana with several other individuals from the college. Because they were so impressed with Lana's intellectual promise and potential, both professors wrote her recommendation letters, which helped Lana gain admittance to Princeton. The other representatives Lana met with were equally impressed; they sent correspondence directly to the admissions office on her behalf. Lana's visit was personalized to her goals and contacts, and therefore, it was a super high-impact and worthwhile experience.

By contrast, Neil connected with key college personnel on a more casual tour of his future school: Dartmouth. Whereas Lana had a carefully pre-arranged visit, Neil's trip to Dartmouth was not so formal; he was one of many future students touring that day. But what he did do was some pre-planning, and he contacted campus representatives ahead of his visit. Neil played high school golf and thought he might be interested in joining the college team. He asked the coach for a meeting and the coach agreed. The meeting ended up lasting over an hour; the golf coach was extraordinarily generous with his time. Later, he wrote Neil a glowing recommendation letter. It's no surprise that Neil got into Dartmouth.

LESSONS FROM LANA'S AND NEIL'S STORIES

Make the most of your college visits.
- Lana had pre-arranged meetings with professors and key university personnel; Neil's visit with the golf coach

wasn't quite as well planned out but ended up being highly impactful. By meeting with school VIPs, Lana and Neil maximized their time on their college campus visits. When they applied, admissions reps were able to see Lana and Neil in three dimensions rather than flatly represented on an online application.

• Did Lana benefit from her mother's outreach? Absolutely, just like Neil benefited from his involvement in golf and his potential value to Dartmouth's team. This doesn't negate the bold steps that both Lana and Neil took to reach out. Meeting with reps from your dream school is scary! Too many people don't take this important step; they take themselves out of the running before they even get to the starting line. "I'll probably waste their time," "Why would person XYZ want to meet with me?," "Everyone else who meets with person XYZ must have 1600s on their SATs," etc. You have to believe you are *worthy* to meet with these individuals, who are people just like you. I'll give you more advice on how to connect with college reps and set up such meetings at the end of this chapter.

Relationship building with college representatives is icing on the cake. *You're* the cake.
• Both Lana and Neil were excellent college applicants, regardless of whatever connections they did or did not make. Relationship building with key personnel added to *what they had already done* in their pursuits of a great college education. This approach to relationship building is the opposite of schmoozing. Schmoozing

implies that a student coasts into their chosen university on charm, money, Mom and Dad's connections, or some combination of the three. Let's say that Lana sat back and let her mom ask all the questions; or that Neil got fidgety after a half hour with the golf coach and was glancing at his phone, with half an hour of their meeting yet to go. Do you think Lana's future professors or the Dartmouth golf coach would have written such warm, enthusiastic recommendations?

• No way. College professors are busy; they don't write recommendation letters for students unless they really mean it—unless the students have made a genuine impression. Lana and Neil were engaged, enthusiastic, and courteous during their meetings. This was the icing on the cake that was *them*—the excellent students they already were, the hard work they'd put in over the last several years of college prep.

Don't be afraid to ask.

• When Neil asked to meet with the golf coach, he thought it would be a 15-minute sit-down—30 minutes tops. Imagine his surprise when the golf coach devoted more than an hour to him and then was so generous in his letter. Had Neil been afraid to ask for the meeting, he would have forfeited what turned out to be a distinct advantage in his acceptance to Dartmouth.

• Oprah Winfrey said, "You get in life what you have the courage to ask for." As I'll talk about in the last section of this chapter, there are "big" asks and "small" asks that you may make of reps from your chosen college. But if you make *no* asks, then that's what you get: nothing. If you approach key personnel in the right way, you'll be surprised by what these individuals say *yes* to. Put your best foot forward: that is, do the work to show up as the best possible applicant you can be. Be courteous, giving, and interested in more than a "you give me this, I'll give you that" relationship; then, ask for what you need. Show up in this way and people will be happy to help you.

Practical Tips on Connecting With Key University Personnel

Ready to start applying the "it's who knows you" principle to your college search?

First: consider your top-choice colleges, places where you want to do further outreach with key reps. Use the tools, reflection questions, and exercises in this book to check in with yourself and make sure you feel a sense of *belonging* at these universities. If you're not actually interested in attending, then outreach is a waste of both your and the college faculty members' time.

Once you've narrowed down your list to places in which you are truly interested, do the following:

Identify opportunities through which you can connect with reps from your chosen college.

These may include: college tours, summer programs, and alumni networks. Go online and see what's coming up. The more high-touch your connection with the school, the more context you'll have for building a relationship. That means it's better to go on a tour than simply attend an open house in your town—but don't sweat it if travel and tours are not in your budget. If you're starting from zero (no family history at the school and no way to travel there), connect with an alumni network and ask to be put in touch with someone at the school via an active alumnus.

Set up meetings (online or in person) with administrators at the college.

This sounds scary—but it doesn't have to be! Let's say you want to explore a school's music program and ask a question of a professor, yet you're unable to travel to the school and ask in person. You may send an email that sounds like this:

Hello! I'm really interested in the music department at [school XYZ]. My experience is [briefly summarize; maybe include a link to an online portfolio]. I think I want to pursue conducting as a career and would love to know which classes could best prepare me for that track. Would you have ten minutes for a phone call to discuss?

This email does three things.

Number one: It's courteous and establishes you as a friendly person. **Number two:** It shows your relevant interest and experience in the subject matter (i.e., you didn't pick up this subject yesterday). **Number three:** It asks a specific question as well as provides a time frame for the answering of that question (ten minutes). The professor knows you and your parents aren't expecting her to give up a half day of research and instruction to answer a question that just popped into your head.

If you take this approach, phone calls are great. Skype or Zoom calls are even better! Don't underestimate the relationship-building currency you can generate from a face-to-face meeting, even if it's via the computer.

When you make an in-person connection, work it for all it's worth.

Let's say you attend an info session where you meet an admissions counselor. When you get home, don't wait; send a quick follow-up email to the counselor reminding him of your meeting, thanking him for his time, and opening the door for future communication. If you're planning on touring a college and want to connect with a particular professor, send an email ahead of time: "I'll be visiting your class on Wednesday and am so excited, as I'm interested in majoring in XYZ. If it's all right with you, I'd like to say hello after class."

These small steps cost you nothing but a few extra minutes; yet use them, and you will stand out *miles* ahead of the competition. The more you connect with people from your chosen college, the more three-dimensional your application becomes. Don't settle for being another faceless applicant in a sea of thousands—go for personal touches wherever you can. Be creative, be bold, be polite. You'll be surprised at what doors open for you.

Don't let these connections go to waste: use them in your application essay.

Colleges want to see your "demonstrated interest" in attending their institution. Think of making connections and relationship building with key personnel as gathering evidence for why you want to attend your top-choice university. Once you gather the evidence for yourself, present that evidence in your essay. Mention a particularly enlightening conversation with a professor, an alumni event that gave you a new perspective, or a new insight you garnered from sitting in on a professor's class . . . anything that made a real impact on you and shows a high level of demonstrated interest to counselors.

Whatever you do, don't assume that anyone besides you knows or cares about your efforts to connect with school personnel. Put that info where it counts—in your essay. If you have a university rep backing you via a recommendation letter, all the better . . . but don't leave this to chance, either! If you've built a great relationship with someone at your top-choice school, *ask* for the glowing review. The worst someone can say is no. Even if you don't have that review, you can still share your takeaways from the conversation in your essays—especially your supplemental essays targeted directly to the colleges of your choosing.

There is an art to cultivating connections and building relationships—but it's not rocket science. Make time-appropriate contact in conjunction with your school tours or other obvious touch points. Make small asks when appropriate, after you've first established yourself as a kind and courteous human being. View relationship building as a long-term game rather than a one-off transaction (i.e., "I email you, you get me what I want"). In order for this to work, you have to genuinely care about the people with whom you connect. Sure, you have an underlying goal: admission to your top-choice school. But don't be so focused on your own admission that you forget to be kind to the people who can *help* you achieve that goal. Remember: they see thousands of kids just like you every year. You're not a rare orchid, however impressive your credentials. How will you be remembered? Will the people at your top-choice school *smile* when they think of you?

The more people invested in the fate of your application, the better. Go out on a limb and make those connections with people who can help you. By acting on the advice in this chapter, you'll be taking a simple step that will help you rocket past the competition. It's worth it—and so are you.

EIGHT

Go Big or Go Home

Life is either a daring adventure or nothing at all.

—HELEN KELLER

Think about a time when you went after something because you *kind of* wanted it. Maybe you thought this particular thing would look good on your high school resume; maybe your mom or dad urged you to do it. You went through the motions, put in a little effort—and when you *didn't* get that thing, you breathed a sigh of relief.

Now think about a time when you *really* wanted something. You were obsessed. You ate, slept, and dreamed this goal: failure was not an option. You knew that if someone told you *no*, you'd keep going anyway. Whether you entered your dream through the front door, side door, back door, a window, or the chimney—you were determined to find a way into this particular reality.

When you approach your dreams with that kind of energy, nothing can stop you.

That was me with NYU. Getting into NYU meant more than *anything* else: this goal was my obsession throughout sophomore, junior, and senior year. I would have done anything. If someone had told me to climb Mt. Everest and my admission was guaranteed, I would have hightailed it to REI to browse their hiking boots and walking sticks. Nothing was going to stop me from making the biggest impression possible—that's why when I finally got my admission letter, I sobbed on the floor. It's a powerful thing when your deepest-held dream comes true.

I'm grateful that I wanted admission to NYU so badly, but obsessive desire isn't always healthy, and it's not sustainable over the course of a lifetime. You can't go *so hard* all the time: you'll burn out (or give yourself a heart attack . . . or pneumonia in my case). But for those three years, my desire for NYU was a galvanizing force. It clarified all of my decisions: Will this get me closer to NYU or further away from NYU? Having such a clear picture of what I wanted was a gift. I didn't have "decision fatigue"; my mind wasn't pulled in 20 different directions by the schools I *could* attend. There was one school I was *going* to attend: my single-mindedness produced incredible focus.

Maybe you have several colleges on your list of dream schools. Maybe you're like me, and there's only ever been one choice. Either mindset is okay. What matters is that the schools you're applying to are places where you can envision yourself belonging (and you do need some backups, too!). I hope you've eliminated from your list schools that were only there because of other people's expectations. Look at your list. When you imagine yourself as part of the student body of each school you've identified, do you smile? Do you think you'll be happy there?

Only consider colleges that meet this standard. If you haven't done so already, rank your choices. How badly do you want your top choice? What's the alternative to *not* getting into your number one pick? With your desire crystal clear, it's time to pull out all the stops. Go BIG in your pursuit of your dream—you have nothing to lose.

In this chapter, we'll meet individuals who went big as they made the transition from high school to college. These people laid it all on the line. They knew that going big had no downside—the worst that could happen was a rejection letter from their top-choice schools. If you're like I was in high school (i.e., obsessively fixated on one school only), a rejection from your dream school may seem like a fate worse than death—but it's *not*. If NYU had rejected me, I would have gone on breathing. But I didn't want to leave anything to chance: I wanted to do *everything* I could to get my *yes*.

No matter the outcome, going big on your dreams is always a good idea. In the pursuit of a big goal, you become a better person. You see the pathway toward your goal and find the courage to take the first step—as well as the stamina to persevere in the face of disappointments. Let's face it: sometimes going BIG for a goal . . . sucks. You have to make sacrifices. There will be plenty of times when no one around you "gets it"—when people give you side-eye for your single-mindedness. Like when . . .

- your friends are out partying on a Saturday night and you're in your room, going over your essay for the hundredth time.
- you're putting in extra hours for test prep to get your score up another 50 points.
- you're the youngest person at an alumni gathering—your friends ask you why you want to hang with "old people," but you know you can make important connections at the event.
- you spend your Saturdays combing the internet for more scholarships to apply for.

If you've found yourself in any of the above scenarios—with your friends on the sidelines rolling their eyes—take a deep breath. You're in good company. Think of the work you're doing right now as training. Admission to your dream college is just one of many goals that you'll set in your lifetime: you are training yourself to be a person who has big goals and goes BIG in the pursuit of them. Keep that up for a lifetime and your success is guaranteed. Consider this quote from Brené Brown:

Truth and courage aren't always comfortable, but they're never weakness.

If you want an okay life, stay where you're comfortable: don't grow and stretch and do the things that make you terrified. If you want a *great* life, get outside your comfort zone as often as possible. Here's another quote from a great mind:

*I see it, I want it . . . I dream it, I work hard, I grind
till I own it.*

—BEYONCÉ

You have nothing to lose and everything to gain by going big.

. . . .

Dorie Clark: Making a BIG Move at a Young Age

Dorie Clark is an entrepreneurial powerhouse. She's a strategy consultant, speaker, and writer with three books and counting to her name. Dorie has been called an "expert at self-reinvention and helping others make changes in their lives" by the *New York Times*.

But growing up, Dorie felt like a misfit in her small town in North Carolina. The town is a draw to a particular type of person: golfers. Dorie's parents moved there so they could golf more—people from all over the country do the same! But Dorie wasn't interested in golf; she wanted exposure to more cultural activities and intellectual stimulation. In her town, those things just weren't on the menu. As a young gay woman, Dorie's differences from her parents and peers became even more pronounced.

In Dorie's freshman year of high school—which turned out to be her *only* year of high school—Dorie dropped out of the social scene. She realized the people she was around weren't "her people"; she stopped making an effort to connect with her peers, who clearly wanted different things. Instead of hanging out or going to parties, Dorie would stay home and read magazines. Dorie's mom became worried she was depressed. In reality, Dorie wasn't depressed: she was in the wrong place.

Dorie came out to herself when she was 13. At 14, she took the big step of coming out to her mom. Speaking her truth allowed Dorie to conceptualize a plan to leave her town and move closer to the life she envisioned for herself. Actually, she conceptualized *several* plans.

"I came up with a plan A, plan B, and plan C, all of which were aimed at that goal [of leaving my hometown]," said Dorie. "Plan A, which I fortunately was able to operationalize, was to go to college early. I enrolled in Mary Baldwin College (now Mary Baldwin University). I went when I was 14. It was the best thing that could have happened for me. My mom was really sad because I was an only child and I think she was not counting on me going away early, but I was very resolute and she was supportive."

Imagine how scared Dorie must have been to make this move, even though she knew it was the big step she needed to make. Think back to your 14-year-old self—how would that kid have fared in college? While Dorie's classmates prepared for sophomore year, Dorie was readying herself to attend college hundreds of miles away. At any point, Dorie could have said "never mind." Going to college as a new teenager is a crazy idea; Dorie might have decided it was *too* crazy—and after all, what was the rush?

Yet Dorie sensed that if she was going to fulfill her potential, she needed to make a big move—and she made it. Dorie's first big step—starting college at 14—was followed by other big steps. Dorie graduated from Smith College at 18 and got a master's from Harvard by 20, when most of her peers were still in their sophomore year of undergrad. From there, Dorie entered the workforce and underwent multiple career evolutions, from journalist to nonprofit leader to award-winning three-time author, to speaker and coach. Dorie even produced a multiple-Grammy-winning jazz album!

Pro tip: there is no career track for journalist-nonprofit leader-author-speaker-coach-music producer. Each new reinvention was the result of Dorie following her intuition and taking bold action. Imagine how things might have turned out if Dorie had not taken the big, scary step of beginning college so early. She was willing to go out on a limb for the future she envisioned, even though those around her didn't understand it. Dorie didn't let the negative projections and limiting beliefs of others hold her back. Dorie was so in love with where she was going; she took big steps—followed by quantum leaps—to get there.

LESSONS FROM DORIE'S STORY

- **Don't be afraid to make a big move.** Dorie sensed that to become the person she wanted to be, she needed to leave her hometown. She could have chosen a college near her home or even in her state of North Carolina. Yet Dorie had the courage to leave. Sometimes big goals require a big change of scenery.

What about you—how necessary is leaving home for your personal development? Only you know your situation: everyone's needs are different. Yet if you sense in your heart that leaving home will be the best thing for you, do it. You may disappoint people, just like Dorie's mom was upset by her move. But you owe it to yourself to test your boundaries and see what you can learn as the result of making a big move.

- **Set goals—and prepare for them not to work out.** Dorie set a plan A, plan B, and plan C to get out of her town and get a better education. If her first-choice plan hadn't worked out, she'd have had another path to follow to achieve her dreams. You too can make contingency plans for your future—if the first pathway isn't available, make adjustments and try something else. Things change, and it pays to be flexible. Give yourself more than one option for what a successful future could look like: but once you've identified your deepest desire, *don't hold back*. When you're working toward a big goal, develop tunnel vision. Don't think about your contingency plans just yet; go hard toward your number one goal. If it doesn't materialize the way you hoped, *then* move to plan B—and go all in on that, too. Whatever you're working toward, work toward it full out.

- **Take your family into consideration, but don't let them hold you back.** As an only child, Dorie could have easily felt she had to stay behind to protect her parents' feelings. But she knew there was something more important waiting for her, and she knew she couldn't find it at home. While at the time the separation was difficult, Dorie's choices led to her success. If she had stayed where she was, Dorie would never have been able to live out her dreams and become who she was meant to be.

- **Your people are out there.** If you feel like a misfit in your high school and your hometown, *you are not alone.* It's hard to articulate your hopes and desires when they are so at odds with what everyone around you wants. If you're not sure exactly what you *do* want, sometimes all you have to know is *not this.* Not fitting in is tough; maybe like Dorie, you've quit making the effort to connect with others who are not even on your wavelength. If you're LGBTQ or a member of a minority group, as Dorie was, this can be a form of self-protection that you're *entitled* to. It's perfectly okay to not expend energy toward people who may not be safe.

- **But I want to assure you:** *your people are out there.* Go big in your search for them, even if you have to take a drastic measure like Dorie did. As Dorie would tell you: it's worth it. You deserve to be surrounded by amazing people who see *your* amazing-ness. Finding your people will help you go the distance and achieve your dreams. They're out there: when you find them, you'll be so glad for all the big steps you took that brought you together.

. . . .

Client Story: To Stand Out to Your Dream School, Would You Write a Whole Book? Mike Did.

Mike was a junior when he and I started working together. Mike had fantastic test scores and a stellar GPA. But that's not always enough to secure a ticket to a top-tier college; the admissions committee wants to see students who are leaders in their own unique capacity. This is why so many students overload their schedules with extracurricular activities—they're caught up in the Impressiveness Paradox.

Remember the Impressiveness Paradox from the introduction to this book? That's when students try too hard to *seem* impressive. They cram their resumes full of credentials and activities, some that have little to no meaning for them. The result: college admissions counselors see through the showy façade and *aren't* impressed. Rather, they wish the student had picked a lane and gone down it full tilt.

Mike was different than the student in the Impressiveness Paradox trap. He spent his time on activities he actually enjoyed—skateboarding, playing in a band, writing his blog. Because of his enthusiasm and commitment to activities that were fun for him, Mike was impressive just as he was. Yet he needed to package that impressiveness in a way that would wow the admissions committee of his top-choice college: Pitzer.

Since Mike liked to write, I suggested a bold idea: Had he ever considered writing a book?

There were a number of reasons that this suggestion was . . . a little crazy. Mike had never written a book before and didn't know the first thing about self-publishing. We were working with a quick timeline; it was February, and we decided that the book should be complete by September. Not to mention that the book would be written in English—Mike's first language was Chinese!

Yet Mike was game. The first step Mike took was assembling people to review and edit his work. To his surprise, a dozen of his peers jumped at the chance to be a part of Mike's project. Mike selected two reviewers to get his work in tip-top shape. Mike set up a timeline with his reviewers and turned in each chapter at the agreed-upon date. In addition to helping Mike get his book ready for publication, the review group became a club that Mike launched all on his own. Rather than try to fit into an existing high school activity to round out his impressiveness for admissions counselors, Mike created an activity—and thus stood out *more* than if he'd been a seat-filler in another group.

Over the summer, Mike navigated the world of Amazon self-publishing. This presented a unique set of challenges and headaches. Mike lived in China—he had to educate himself on the U.S. Amazon platform. But Mike didn't let the country-to-country red tape stop him: he persevered with the help of supportive friends and community members who were invested in his success.

Mike's drive and self-starter quality impressed the admissions team at Pitzer College. Mike chose Pitzer because he wanted a liberal arts education with a West Coast vibe where his creativity and free-spirited nature could be nurtured. Pitzer's acceptance rate is 13.5 percent—yet Mike earned a spot in the incoming freshman class. His willingness to stretch himself and try something out of the box paid off.

Mike is a great example of someone who charted his own course to success rather than box-checking his way through high school. He went BIG—bigger than he'd ever gone before—to achieve his dreams. If you were going to go as big as you could possibly go . . . what would it look like?

LESSONS FROM MIKE'S STORY

* **Choose your "thing" and do it well.** You don't have to join every after-school activity and attend every club meeting to be a knockout candidate. Instead of loading your resume with an arm's-length of checkbox activities, choose one thing to do well. You are better off creating your own extracurricular activity and producing something tangible from it (like a book) than joining the debate team, yearbook, student council, and so on. What's your "thing"? What would going *big* in that one area look like?

* **If you're an artist:** could you revitalize a shabby area of your town by painting a mural? If your interest lies in web design, could you create an app that helps the people in your immediate community? If you're an aspiring businessperson, what business could you start *right now*? Your efforts don't have to be perfect—in fact, they won't be. Kick "perfect" to the curb—it doesn't exist. What counts is that you make a big plan and *do it* to the best of your ability. Do this, and you'll be miles ahead of the applicant who came up with a million perfect plans but never acted on any of them.

- **Big goals are made up of tiny steps.** If Mike had merely had the goal "write a book," without further breaking that goal into tiny steps, the book never would have been written. Mike recognized that if he was going to achieve his goal, he had to take it piece by piece. Mike faced plenty of challenges en route to his finished book. Challenge number one: writing a book in his second language. Most people who want to write a book in their native language never do it! Yet Mike persevered and got the job done. Challenge number two: actually writing the book. Mike enlisted help for this step: he knew that to go from idea to published book in six months, he would need people to hold his feet to the fire. Mike enlisted his friends as accountability partners and did whatever it took to meet each deadline he set. Challenge number three: figuring out the intricacies of online publishing. For this challenge, Mike enlisted his family to help him learn the ins and outs of the U.S. Amazon platform. This step was time-consuming and often just plain boring. Many times, the individual steps to your dream don't look exciting—they look tedious and yawn inducing. How do you move toward your big dream when the steps leading to it aren't any fun?
- **Newsflash:** a whole lot of boring steps will stand between you and your dreams for the rest of your life. Author, speaker, and creativity diva Elizabeth Gilbert says that the job of "writer"—a role that has brought

her tremendous success and is the fulfillment of a life-long dream—is boring 90 percent of the time.[1] Your dream doesn't always *feel* like your dream! Here's the difference between those who achieve big success and those who settle for an "okay" life somewhere in the middle: big achievers have patience to do the boring stuff others don't have time for. To achieve the impossible, break the impossible goal down into tiny steps—and keep going when those steps aren't any fun.

• **Enlist the help of others.** People have a false idea of authors: that authors shut themselves in attics and avoid human contact in order to write their books. Yet this is exactly opposite of how Mike wrote his book. Mike created a support team that held him accountable for writing deadlines. This team also offered feedback. Assembling his team was a scary step that was crucial to Mike's success (would *you* be willing to let friends read your book when you'd never written one before?). Yet Mike moved past fear and got the support he needed. Once the book was finished, Mike leaned on his family to help him self-publish. In achieving his goal, Mike was never the "solitary genius."

• **To recap the last chapter:** the more people at your top-choice school who are invested in the fate of your application, the better your chances. The same principle applies here. There's an African proverb: "If you want to go fast, go alone. If you want to go

far, go together." It's *scary* to let those close to us in
on our deepest-held dreams. What if those dreams
don't come true? Will we look foolish in front of our
friends and loved ones?

• Yet people who achieve lasting success overcome this
fear and lean on others as they chase their dreams.
Enlisting help doesn't mean that you blab your deepest desires to strangers on the street. Think about
your circle: Who has your back? Know the people
who'll be rooting for you, no matter what. Let them
in on your big dreams—they can help you or point
you to others who can. Believe that you can achieve
whatever you set your mind to, and love yourself no
matter what. If you're not judging yourself, you don't
fear the judgment of others.

Exercise: What Would Going Big
Look Like for You?

Time to go for broke and leave it all on the table. Nothing
ventured, nothing gained: if you want your top-choice school
to take you seriously, start by taking yourself seriously. Do the
thing you're scared to do. Make the connections you're scared
to make. Be so irresistible you *force* your dream school to take
another look at your application.

We all fight with the urge to stay small and not take up
space. We think: "Who am *I* to have that?" But instead of
asking "why me?" change the question: "Why *not* me?" Other
people have achieved what you want to achieve. They are just

like you. The only things separating you from your wildest dreams are your thoughts. So think big and play big—make a habit of bigness, and nothing can stop you.

1. To identify your big, bold move that will *wow* your favorite school's admissions committee, grab a journal and write your answers to the following questions:
2. What are your interests and special talents? Make a list.

Now, circle the one that is most exciting to you.

3. If you were to go *all in* on the activity that you circled, what would that look like for you?
   a. Put on your own recital in an interesting venue. Sell tickets and create an experience for your guests.
   b. Create and sell a product that helps customers achieve a desired goal.
   c. Organize and throw a fundraiser for a cause you're passionate about.
   d. Write a book!
4. Once you've identified your big idea, break it into smaller steps. What's the *first* step you need to take toward your big plan?
5. What social proof do you need to showcase your big move? This may be a video, website, book, or something else. Think of what you need—and who can help you create it.

6. Who can help you achieve your big goal? Brainstorm
   names, then begin assembling your team!

You either walk inside your story and own it or you
stand outside your story and hustle for your worthiness.
—BRENÉ BROWN

You don't want to look back on your college application
journey and regret playing small. Playing big is not about doing
everything: it's about identifying your superpower and doubling
down on it. Don't hold back! Give the world the gift of your
greatness. In going big, you'll show yourself what you're capable
of and inspire others, too. Stretching beyond what you think
is possible is always worth it: you don't know what the ripple
effects of your bold action will be. But I can guarantee that *you'll*
be changed—for the better—by reaching for the next level.

Go for it.

Self-Care Tips for College Admissions Season

You've got it circled on the calendar: the day you'll hear *yes*
or *no* from your top-choice college. December, late March,
or early April—just thinking of those times may send a chill
down your spine. You imagine the elation you'll feel if the
school of your dreams opens its arms to you. And if they
say *no* . . . the thought is too painful to consider.

I get it. My desire for NYU made me a nervous wreck. You
may feel that you have no other choice than to obsess about
your application—*Who's looking at it right now? That thing my*

teacher said in the reference letter could make them think I'm lazy. I should have picked a different story for my essay!—but I want to tell you that there is another way.

You do not *have* to make yourself sick awaiting news from your top-choice college. Dread and foreboding are entirely optional. There is a healthier way to deal with your stress than to stare catatonically at your phone waiting for the magic email, gnawing your fingernails until they're gone. Whatever your dream college says, these are your final months in high school. Enjoy them, please! You will never be where you are right now, in the place you call home with the friendships you've built over the last four years—or maybe even over the course of your lifetime—again.

You *can* enjoy this time in your life. You do not have to become a slave to your anxiety. In fact, please don't—besides making yourself sick, you'll make your friends and family want to pull their hair out. Below are tips on how you can take care of yourself *right now*, even before you get your perfect *yes*:

1. Get Enough Sleep.

The American Academy of Pediatrics recommends that teenagers get between eight and ten hours of sleep each night. Yet many teens fall far short of that amount. In one study conducted by a nonprofit affiliated with Stanford University's Graduate School of Education, 145,000 students were studied; they averaged about 6.5 hours of sleep a night.[2] You've probably experienced the effects of not sleeping enough: grumpiness, overeating or undereating, getting sick and stressed more easily. Less than 19 percent of the students studied got a full eight hours; less than 4 percent got nine or more hours of sleep a night.

In addition to the negative effects listed above, here's another: less sleep makes you dumber. The final 90 minutes of your sleep cycle helps your brain to remember things and it also primes you to learn new things. Your memory and learning capabilities don't work properly if you don't sleep.

"Get more sleep? You should tell my teachers to give less homework!" If you're thinking this, I totally get it—and I feel for you. The amount of homework teenagers are expected to do each night has gotten completely out of hand—but that's a topic for another book. Let's focus on what we can control. Would it be possible for you to go to bed 15 minutes earlier, five days in a row? Could you then move your bedtime forward by five minutes (20 minutes earlier than your current bedtime)? Or does the idea of having a bedtime sound totally nuts to begin with?

If you don't have a bedtime for yourself, try to implement one. Experiment with moving it up: How do you feel after 6.5 hours of sleep, 6.75 hours, 7 . . . and so on? Note your stress levels and overall happiness the following day. Your goal is to *feel* good so that you can handle whatever stressors come your way. Find your feel-good sleep number and do your best to maintain it.

2. Take Care of Your Body.

Sleeping enough is one way to take care of your body—and it's a big one, so we started there. Don't forget the other basics either, like:

- Drink plenty of water. However much you're drinking right now, could you up it by 8 oz. daily?
- Exercise a few times a week, in whatever way is fun for you.
- Eat healthy foods: fruits, vegetables, nuts, protein. Limit overly processed foods or products that are high in sugar.

Do I sound like your mom here? Maybe (and full disclosure, I *am* a mom). But these little actions make a big difference in your overall health and happiness. When you're fixated on the future (e.g., when you'll hear from your dream college), it's easy to forget basic maintenance required for your well-being. But forget these fundamentals and you'll find yourself slipping into stress.

When anxiety starts to creep, practice the HALT method. Ask yourself: "Am I Hungry, Angry, Lonely, or Tired?" This simple question may give you the answers you need: to calm your racing thoughts, maybe all you need is a juicy hamburger or a long nap. Keep in mind this quote, speaker anonymous: "Drink water. Get sunlight. You're basically a houseplant with more complicated emotions."

3. Limit Social Media.

This may be the hardest tip of all—and thus the most important. How much time do you spend on social media a day? Activate your phone's screen time feature to learn the actual number. If the number is high, my bet is that you're not as happy as you could be.

This bet is backed by science: in two studies surveying over 500,000 teens, teens with higher usage of social media were more likely to report mental health issues.[3] Students who spent more time engaged in sports and other face-to-face interactions with peers reported *fewer* mental health difficulties.

It makes sense. If you're feeling down and spend an hour scrolling Instagram, how do you feel afterward? Probably even worse—everyone's lives, no matter how they actually are, *appear* perfect on Instagram. When you compare yourself to the perfect images you find online, your sadness becomes even more pronounced. On the flip side, what if you're super happy about something? Go to social media and stay a little too long—you'll find someone who has something even *better* than you. Suddenly the thing you were happy about doesn't look so great; you lose your appreciation for where you are right now.

Here's where HALT comes into play again: are you lonely when you hop on social media? You'll feel even lonelier after scroll time. I'm so glad social media wasn't a thing when I was in high school. If I'd seen videos of kids getting into NYU on Instagram—thousands of them, available 24/7—I would have been even more of an anxious mess. And I would have felt so lonely seeing all those kids achieve the thing I wanted.

Notice your patterns. When are you tempted to reach for your phone? How could you interrupt that pattern and replace it with a habit that will make you happier? Read a book, go for a run, bake cupcakes, sit under a tree: how you interrupt unhealthy social media tendencies doesn't matter, just so long as you do. Prioritize your mental health above all else. Your mental health is way more important than liking all your friends' posts or counting *your* likes. It's okay to be behind on your feed: what matters more is your happiness.

4. Lean Into Friendships.

The studies I mentioned reported that students with higher levels of peer interaction had better mental health. Now is the time to hang with people who have your back. Ask yourself: Who do you enjoy hanging out with the most? What could you and your tribe do together that has *nothing* to do with college applications?

If you hang out with your friends and someone (or you!) brings up stress about college, do your best to shut that down. If you're a nervous wreck, don't hang around people who amplify your nervous energy. Make *fun* the primary goal of your friend hangouts. Only give your time to people who understand you and will celebrate you, win or lose.

Likewise, celebrate your friends on their big wins. If you and your BFF are applying to the same college and they get their acceptance letter while you're still waiting—or after you've gotten a *no*—respond the way you hope your friend would respond if the situation were reversed. No matter your feelings on the inside, be the bigger person: have your friends' backs, just as they've got yours. Having good relationships is more important than having a degree from the most prestigious school on your list. College is only four years: friendships could be for life. Appreciate the people in your life; spend time with them; have *fun*. Savor these high school days and the people who make them special. They won't come around again.

As stress-filled as these days may seem, you will look back on them and miss them. Enjoy them *now*. Remember this quote from the renowned Buddhist teacher Thich Nhat Hanh (emphasis mine):

We are very good at preparing *to live, but not very good at* living. *We know how to sacrifice ten years for a diploma, and we are willing to work very hard to get a job, a car, a house, and so on. But we have difficulty remembering that we are alive in the present moment, the only moment there is for us to be alive.*

College will be here soon; for now, appreciate where you are, how far you've come, and all that lies ahead. Take care of yourself. Breathe. Smile. Know that where you are now is exactly where you're meant to be.

NINE

When the Dream Isn't
So Dreamy

Once you get accepted into your dream college, all your problems disappear and your deepest wishes come true. Right?

By now, I hope you hear the heavy sarcasm in those words! We've talked about how college is just the beginning of your journey to your best self. Acceptance is the *beginning* of the beginning—making it into your dream college is great, but you have four years ahead of you. What are you going to make of that time? Getting into your top-choice school is a huge win—but how are you going to set yourself up so that you can keep on winning?

On the flip side, hearing a *no* from your dream school is not the end of the road, either. If you're determined to have a fantastic college experience, no matter the university, then that's what you'll have. It's up to you to make the most of the situation, no matter where you end up. The "dream" of your dream college isn't always so ideal—as you'll see from my experience at NYU.

Remember how I obsessed over NYU with every fiber of my being? Once my anxiety and pneumonia-ridden application process was complete and I finally got my *yes*, I relaxed a little. (The truth was, I should have committed to relaxing and enjoying myself more from the start. There was no need to make myself sick—getting pneumonia didn't help my application.) Yet even though NYU was my dream school, the reality of *being* a new college student was anything but dreamy.

Move-in day at Rubin Hall was chaotic. I and hundreds of my fellow incoming freshmen waited in a long line to get checked in; then the elevators broke, and my parents and I had to carry heavy luggage up five flights of stairs. (I had my huge stereo—a very important accessory back then, especially for a music business major!) Not only was I a sweaty mess because of the lack of air conditioning; I also had to make the mental adjustment of living with a roommate after 18 years as an only child accustomed to plenty of personal space.

But these "problems" were insignificant compared to a harsh reality I was soon to face. During the second week of classes, I was in the middle of economics when the first of two planes struck the Twin Towers on September 11, 2001. Terrorists had hijacked four planes in midflight; two of these planes flew into the two skyscrapers at the World Trade Center in New York City. These towers were just two miles from NYU and within sight of Washington Square Park, the university's central green space.

At the time, I was inside a building and traveling from

my 8:00 a.m. economics class to my 9:30 music theory class; somehow, I didn't hear the planes strike the towers or the many people screaming on the streets. I didn't know we were under attack. When I heard about the attack in music theory class, I thought it must be a mistake. It couldn't be true. My memories after that class are foggy. I don't remember if we were released from class early or if we stayed the whole time. I do remember eventually walking back to Rubin Hall by myself, my head down as low as possible. I didn't want to see anything. But I couldn't hide from the penetrating smell, a combination of melting steel, glass, and bodies.

Back at the dorm there was a long line of people waiting to use the pay phone to call their parents. Many cell phones weren't working, and the phone lines in the dorms were only intermittently active. Luckily, I had a cell phone that allowed me to reach my parents so I could tell them I was okay. I sat alone in my dorm for the rest of the day. The following day, I made the trip back to the suburbs for a long weekend away from NYC.

I knew I was lucky to survive the Twin Towers' collapse. I also realized I was fortunate that my dorm did not directly face the towers (some did). In the coming weeks, many students I talked with spoke of an intention to transfer; plenty actually did. I even thought about transferring myself. College was supposed to be a bridge between the "real world" and home—not a $30,000-plus ticket into a war zone.

My freshman year continued to be a struggle. Not only was I struggling to make sense of 9/11—I was also adjusting to the time pressures imposed by classes, activities, and clubs. I was under the mistaken impression that freshmen had to have an internship; thus, I interned at *Billboard Magazine* and spent my days searching the internet for instances of copyright infringement, wondering why someone of my intelligence level was involved in such menial work. I was beginning to have doubts about the path I'd once felt so certain of. Day to day, the work I was engaged in felt insignificant, like a giant waste of time.

Besides that internship, I didn't participate much beyond what was required. I did okay—not great—in my classes. Rather than build relationships with peers, explore new interests through clubs, and do the sometimes uncomfortable work of figuring out who I was and what I wanted, I spent most of my mental energy pursuing a boyfriend from back home. I talked to him at night and traveled to see him on the weekends. All of these conflicting engagements made it impossible for me to be fully present now that I was *finally* at NYU.

Fortunately for me, the boyfriend broke up with me early in sophomore year. This freed me up mentally; I began to think of new possibilities for myself. For the first time I began psychotherapy, a tool I highly recommend for people of any age. By giving myself space to emotionally process my circumstances, and by getting distance from the relationship and from 9/11, I became more empowered to dive in fully to my NYU experience. I made a commitment to myself to pursue clubs and activities that I found interesting. I took on several pursuits all at once, including our college's programming board, the residence life board, Hillel, and the music business program's newly formed student ambassador board. Little did I know then that the student ambassador board would provide the spark for my future career in higher education—a field I didn't even know existed until college.

The work I did on the ambassador board was especially exciting to me. My peers and I were able to collaborate with faculty to implement a number of department-wide initiatives: these included changing some requirements in the music business program curriculum, organizing program-specific concerts, and being a voice for the student body. I felt like I was contributing, like my presence on the board improved life for students in the music business program—and my life as well. I finally had a sense of purpose for my college experience. Likewise, my experience at Hillel helped me find a community of friends—and, eventually, my husband.

By the time senior year rolled around, I was so *over* wanting to have a career in the music business. Much like my freshman year internship, my subsequent college internships lacked intellectual stimulation . . . and they featured some strange characters. I met one executive who wore pajamas to work. Another supervisor, after a late-night party, invited me to sleep in his bed—with him in it. Nope, nope, nope. This was not my scene.

But it wasn't only the weirdos who turned me off to the music business. All in all, the people in the industry just weren't my people. I never found someone I clicked with; I didn't want to be mentored by any of the professionals around me. I wanted to find a line of work that was more intellectually stimulating (and didn't require me to stay out late every night!). The money wasn't appealing, either; I knew that if I pursued the music business, I'd have to pay a lot of dues to *eventually* earn a meager salary. I don't regret my pivot away from the music business; if I was truly passionate about the field, I would have found a way to make it work. But fortunately, I had other ideas. I decided to change direction.

Because I'd found so much meaning from my time on the student ambassador board, I decided to apply for and enroll at the University of Pennsylvania's master's program in higher education. All of my research showed that this degree path was the way you entered the field, and Penn's program was one of the best. Through this program I landed a couple of pretty good internships on campus, and eventually my first full-time campus job. In my most recent position at the university, I served at Wharton (UPenn's business school) as an academic administrator, pre-college program director, and undergraduate admissions committee liaison. I had toyed with the idea of being an independent college counselor right out of grad school, but I didn't feel I had enough experience to take that step yet. Overseeing the highly selective Wharton pre-college program (called Leadership in the Business World) and being on the Wharton admissions committee brought me full circle back to my high school experience. I remembered when attending NYU was just a high school pipe dream, and I wondered: could I help people who were applying to college? Most importantly, how could I help them not only get into college but figure out who they are and what they want out of work and life?

These questions birthed the work I've been doing since 2014 as an education entrepreneur, college counselor, executive coach, writer, and faculty member. I'm only getting started. Years after my high school pipe dream, I've found my path.

As you prepare for your own college journey, remember that it will be a learning experience—not a perfect experience. Whatever your thoughts about your "dream" school now, soon college won't be a dream: it will be your real life. That means you'll be challenged intellectually, mentally, and emotionally. You'll stretch and grow—and as is the case for every organism on earth, this growth will not always be comfortable. You'll discover more about what you want to do, or get more practice doing what you love. You may not figure out what you want to do until *after* college—and that's okay, too.

Don't put too much pressure on yourself to have the perfect college experience right off the bat. Many people struggle their freshman year. If you're like me, freshman year will look quite different from sophomore, junior, and senior years—and that's a good thing. It can take time to find your people and your path; if you feel lonely and insecure as you begin your college journey, know that you're not alone.

The book *What Made Maddy Run* by Kate Fagan illustrates this truth and its potentially tragic implications. Madison Holleran was a 19-year-old freshman and track team member at the University of Pennsylvania. Maddy was beautiful, popular, fiercely intelligent, and athletic. Penn was her dream school. To friends and those on the outside looking in, Maddy's life looked perfect. She was living her dream and on track for a brilliant future.

Yet Maddy, as revealed in the book, was also deeply insecure and struggling with demons the world did not see. After returning to campus for the spring semester of her freshman year, Maddy committed suicide. Her death sent shockwaves around campus; everyone wanted to know the answer to one question.

Why?

What Made Maddy Run makes the case that there is no one answer but a myriad of contributing factors. The book stresses the importance of mental health services and how vital they are to the health of college students. While we can never know exactly what Maddy was thinking prior to taking her own life, we can view her story with compassion and learn from it. Maddy's story teaches us that, contrary to appearances, we never know what someone might be struggling with. Even if someone (you?) has checked all the boxes and is living the "perfect"—on paper—college experience, reality can be far from perfect. This was certainly true for me; despite achieving my dream of becoming an NYU student, my freshman year was an unsettling, lonely time.

It took time, but things got so much better. If you find yourself in my freshman-year shoes, know that your life can get so much better, too.

College will present a series of ups and downs; you'll be depressed and happy, bored and excited, wildly ambitious and deeply insecure. You will experience every feeling, and they will all belong. College will be the *beginning* of a new life journey—not the pinnacle of your life. And that's exactly how it should be.

In the second half of this book, I'm going to introduce you to people who used college as a launchpad into the lives of their dreams. Some are doing what they originally set out to do on the first day of freshman orientation; the paths of others have diverged wildly from their first intention. Yet all of the people you'll meet are successes in their own right. All are leading lives they find deeply meaningful and are contributing to their communities in profound ways.

Since this section of the book focuses on college and beyond, there won't be stories from teenagers that I've worked with personally. Their stories—like yours—are only in the opening pages; much remains to be written. But you can borrow a page from the playbooks of the luminaries you're about to meet and create the life of your dreams. Ready to learn how to use your college experience to set you up for a whole lifetime of success?

Read on.

Part Two

COLLEGE and BEYOND

**So you got into your dream college!
(Or you didn't.) Now what?**

. . . .

TEN

Don't Take *No* for an Answer

You've got to have faith in what you're
doing and not take no for an answer.

—NIPSEY HUSSLE

Some people just don't know the meaning of the word *no*.

Take toddlers, for example. A toddler asks for a cookie; you say *no*. They ask *again*. Five minutes later, they ask for *two* cookies. Two minutes after that, they ask for three. And what ends up happening? You give the toddler just one cookie—a good bargain, the toddler might say—by the end of the negotiation.

How do toddlers do that? Nobody taught them negotiation tactics; they aren't strategizing about how they can trick Mom or Dad into handing over that Oreo. Toddlers are able to get what they want because they see no reason why they can't have it.

Read that sentence again. I want you to get in touch with your toddler brain. From a toddler's perspective, everything is simple. I see the cookie; I *want* the cookie. It's right there.

Why can't I have it? I know it's yummy; I know I will feel happy when I'm eating it. All Mom has to do is reach over and open the lid to the cookie jar. Simple.

A toddler knows there are no mysterious forces keeping him from the cookie. If he asks and Mom says *no*, the toddler doesn't believe he "wasn't meant" to have the cookie. Eating the cookie is simply a matter of Mom giving him one. And if Mom doesn't, perhaps he'll figure out a way to crawl up on the counter and get one himself when Mom's back is turned.

What if you approached your deepest-held dreams with the same tenacity as a cookie-wanting two-year-old?

Once our brains get a little older, we buy into all the reasons we can't have the thing that we want. If someone tells us *no*, we'll agree with them, no matter what reason we're given. Even more painful, we'll *make up* lots of reasons why this or that authority figure was right to exclude us. In the case of being told *no* by your top-choice college, the reasons may sound something like this: "It must be because my SAT score wasn't high enough." "My parents aren't important enough, I guess." "It's because I choked in my interview; they must think I'm a weirdo."

I get it. It's devastating to hold a dream so close and then have it not come true. It feels personal—like there must be something wrong with you. When our dreams don't materialize, we have a tendency to launch into comparison mode—to look at all the people the dream *did* happen for and list the ways we don't measure up.

But here's some good news: a *no* is not personal, no matter how deeply it cuts. You can sit around, listing all the reasons you *think* you got that no—or you can come to terms with the fact that whoever told you *no* is most likely not thinking about you at all. That's not meant to be depressing—it's meant to be liberating! No committee is obsessing over your personal faults. No one's struck your name from their list with a red marker and written in the margins: "never ever." That's how we *perceive* nos, yet it isn't the truth. If you list all the reasons you were never good enough and mentally sign off on them, you're not just taking yourself out of the race; you're packing up and leaving the stadium.

Leaving the stadium is entirely optional. In fact, you could get right back in the starting blocks and try again. *Most people don't know this.* They think a *no* is a personal judgment against them—and final. I'm here to tell you that neither of those things is true. A *no* is just the starting point. If you believe in your dream hard enough, never allow a *no* to stand between it and you. There is *always* a way around.

In this chapter, we'll meet people who achieved success despite the odds being against them. These individuals were told *no*—yet like the toddler after the cookie, they just kept going. Because of that tenacity, they are now living the life of their dreams.

Olya Hill: A Life Marked by Audacity and Tenacity

Olya Hill grew up in Ukraine, which was part of the USSR during her childhood. When the Soviet Union fell in the early nineties, Olya suddenly became exposed to new people and ideas: visitors moved freely about the former Soviet Union for the first time in her lifetime, and Olya became curious about them. She began to explore other cultures and ideas.

Olya soon realized that she wanted more for her life than was available in the very traditional culture of Ukraine. A trained ballerina, Olya became interested in pursuing contemporary and modern dance. Yet pursuing a career in the arts in the way Olya desired was not a viable option in her home country; Olya was expected to enter a more traditional and stable career. When she was newly 18 years old, Olya left Ukraine for the United States. She knew she could have stayed in her home country and had a good life—yet the life she would live there would not be the life of her dreams. As Olya said: "It wouldn't be me."

Olya's dream was to gain a college education in America. Yet there were many obstacles in her way—most notably, she would need to learn English. Olya enrolled in language schools and took proficiency tests, determined to score high enough that she would be able to comprehend her future college professors. Olya realized that her best bet for obtaining a college education in the States was to find a scholarship.

But as an international student, there was a limited number of scholarships to which Olya could apply. In fact, Olya applied for scholarships for which she was not even eligible and learned this only after she'd already put in long hours working on her apps. Olya could have thrown up her hands and called the whole endeavor a waste of time—but she didn't. She recommitted her focus. Olya began—literally—knocking on doors at multiple colleges and telling various admissions representatives about herself and where she'd come from. Finally, one person at Brigham Young University got curious. An admissions committee rep asked Olya: "Who are you? Why are you always sitting outside my door?" Olya told him her story, and the admissions rep recommended that she try out for the talent scholarship. She applied and was one of *thousands* of applicants. Olya secured the scholarship, attended Brigham Young University and later NYU—and the rest is history.

A former dancer, Olya is today the founder of Living Notes, an entertainment production company, and Instagram @livingnotes, and a single mom (with primary responsibility for seven kids!). Most of the items on her resume didn't even exist when Olya started her career. Yet, using the same tenacity and adaptability that took her from Ukraine to the United States, Olya embraced the new media landscape and created a beautiful life for herself.

LESSONS FROM OLYA'S STORY

- **Don't be afraid to make a big leap.** Olya, along with so many others we've met in this book, took a huge leap with no guarantee of the outcome. On nothing but instinct, Olya moved across the world to a country where she barely spoke the language. From there, she got to work. Olya looked at her end goal—attending a U.S. college—and broke it into steps: 1) Learn English. 2) Complete residency requirements. 3) Apply for scholarships. Had Olya not made such a huge move, perhaps she wouldn't have been as motivated to make it all work out. After all—she couldn't exactly go home and crash on her parents' couch!

Sometimes it's worth it to jump off the deep end; only then can we truly see what we're capable of.

- **Don't give up too soon.** Imagine Olya's disappointment when she learned she'd dedicated so much time and energy applying to scholarships for which she was not even eligible. If Olya was a different sort of person, this might have been the point at which she threw in the towel. After all— couldn't this be a "sign" that she was never supposed to be in the United States and that she should just head home? Yet Olya persevered until she connected with the admissions representative who gave her a lucky break. You never know how close you are to the person or circumstance who will change *everything* for you, so keep going. The only way to fail is to quit.

- **Persistence plus adaptability equals success.** Olya could never have dreamed that she'd become successful as a social media influencer. Literally, she *couldn't* dream it; the job didn't exist in her youth. Yet when she saw the opportunity the influencing space presented, she got to work building her business. Are there unforeseen opportunities in your ecosystem? (There always are!) Be firm in your goals but flexible about how you'll reach them. Know that it's okay to take forks in the road of your career; yet whatever you pursue, don't hold back. Who knows how technology will change in the next ten years, and what changes those opportunities may present for you. Don't fear the wave of change; ride it and have fun.

Are you an international student who finds yourself banging down doors in the United States? Another former international student, Heather Lu-Lasky, was one of the few to land a job at a top investment bank after graduation. Learn how she did it and what blossomed from carving her own path at www.getrealandgetin.com.

. . . .

Aaron Kirman: When Appealing the *No* Works

Aaron Kirman is a millennial real estate professional who has sold *billions*—with a *b*—in real estate. He and his team have the largest market share of luxury living spaces in the country. Aaron has worked with numerous celebrities, including Ariana Grande and Justin Bieber, and is well known for representing some of the most expensive residential properties both nationally and internationally as well as famous historical and architectural landmarks. Looking at all of Aaron's success now, it would be easy to think that Aaron was destined for it—that his ride to the top has somehow been easy and bump free. But that is far from Aaron's reality.

As a young child, Aaron struggled with a learning disability. He was held back in the first grade. Even at such a young age, not moving on to second grade with his peers was a source of deep embarrassment for Aaron. Throughout his academic career, Aaron continued to struggle. He even admitted to cheating his way through school—not behavior to emulate but the reality of how Aaron got his diploma.

Even though high school was difficult, Aaron looked forward to attending college and embracing the full college experience.

Yet he was rejected from all the colleges he applied to. Aaron was excited about leaving home and starting over in a new place—yet no one was willing to give him that fresh start. That's when Aaron decided to take matters into his own hands.

Aaron wrote a letter to the University of Southern California admissions team, citing his failure to get in and his desire that the committee reconsider. Aaron was frank about his academic struggles but also persuasive in assessing his own talent and drive to succeed. He believed the committee got it wrong, and he told them. The committee *did* reconsider; they admitted Aaron in a program for people with learning disabilities under the condition that he participate in Reserve Officers' Training Corps (ROTC), a training ground for college students seeking to serve in the armed forces. The ROTC would pay his college tuition if he participated.

It was a major victory! At least, it appeared like one at the outset. But Aaron quickly discovered that he hated the ROTC program. Participating in the military was not aligned with his personality. Aaron was ultimately kicked out of the ROTC program, which meant he lost his associated scholarship and needed loans to cover his school bills. Aaron entered real estate as a way to pay back his loans—from there, he built his career, selling one house at a time, into the multi-billion enterprise it is today.

Aaron's journey did not move in a straight line, but each juncture was critical to his eventual success. From being told *no* by USC, to appealing successfully, to joining the ROTC program, to getting kicked *out* of the ROTC program—Aaron learned about himself each step of the way. He learned his own persuasive powers, his ability to turn a *no* into a *yes*. He learned that military life is not for him, even when it comes with a college scholarship. He learned that, when the rubber met the road, he *was* capable of making money and paying back his student loans. Each test, whether it resulted in immediate success or failure, was valuable, because it gave him information about what he wanted and what he didn't want for his life.

LESSONS FROM AARON'S STORY

- *No* **is only the final answer if you let it be.** When Aaron wrote his letter to USC asking that they reconsider and admit him, he didn't have a lot of "cred" to back him up. Aaron did not have stellar grades or a special skill the university would view as valuable. All he had was a belief in his own worthiness and a strong desire to begin his college dream. It was enough; Aaron's gumption counted for way more than any other external validator. When your belief in yourself is rock solid, a *no* may knock you off course for a while—but it won't be the end of your road. In the case of college admissions, consider your options; are there any other universities that are especially attractive to you? Are you *relieved* by the *no*? Is the *no* okay, or do you want to put up a fight? Don't be afraid to fight for the things that matter to you.
- **Sometimes you have to find out what you don't want in order to identify what you do want.** Despite Aaron's deep dislike of his military time in the ROTC, the experience provided invaluable information for

him. Aaron learned that, even though ROTC enabled him to attend college for free, it wasn't worth it *to him*. We all have different "acceptability" thresholds. An experience that may be perfectly fine for someone else may prove torturous for you. I think Aaron made the right move by getting out of ROTC, even though it meant he took on student loan debt. Some sacrifice in the short term is worth long-term gains—but submitting to a miserable college experience isn't something I would advise for anyone. The sooner Aaron was able to realize how ill-suited he was for the military, the sooner he was able to get out of there and discover what he truly loved.

- **Pay attention to what you like;** but just as importantly, pay attention to what you *don't* like. This applies for college majors, relationships, jobs, food— anything and everything that makes up a building block in your life. Both sets of data will help you create the life you love.

- **Sometimes it takes a test to discover what you're truly capable of.** Because of Aaron's innate resourcefulness, he didn't despair at the prospect of taking on student loan debt. Rather, he viewed money as a problem to be solved. Aaron knew he had to pay back a $100,000 loan; he went to work as an employee at a real estate agency. A pattern played out: Aaron got fired from *that* job, just as he'd been kicked out of ROTC. Aaron was learning something: he didn't want to work for other people. The path of entrepreneurship was beckoning. The firing was a test, just like getting kicked out of ROTC was a test. Aaron's setbacks at USC were the catalyst for Aaron entering real estate; losing his job at the real estate agency was the catalyst for beginning his own real estate company, which is now worth billions.

- **You are creative and resourceful;** when the rubber meets the road, you may be astounded to learn what you can accomplish. Don't fear tests; embrace them. They may lead you to your destiny.

REFLECTION QUESTIONS

Have you ever had an experience in which you were told *no* but kept going anyway—and eventually achieved your goal? Write about it. Why did you think the person who said *no* got it wrong? What gave you the courage to keep going? How did you feel when you did what someone else said you couldn't?

Remember that you are *powerful.* You can achieve whatever you set your mind to—and if someone tells you *no*, you can find a workaround. Remember: it doesn't matter how many times others tell you *no* as long as you keep saying *yes* to yourself.

Want to build an entrepreneurial empire and see how the experts do it? Then you'll also want to check out the nontraditional college journey of Tom Bilyeu, founder of Quest Nutrition and Impact Theory, at www.getrealandgetin.com.

ELEVEN

Be Open to the New

*To expect the unexpected shows a
thoroughly modern intellect.*

—OSCAR WILDE

If you wish to succeed, keep an open mind and an open heart. A spirit of openness will be one of your most valuable assets as you create your dream life.

I can hear the groans and see the eye rolls. "An open *heart?* How will keeping my heart open get me a 4.0 and the internship I want? What's something practical I can do?"

Yet all the success strategies in the world can't fully prepare you for college. They couldn't prepare *me*—if so, I'd be well into my music business career right now, instead of writing this book for you. My networking, research, trips to NYU, and deep dives into research of the music business industry—none of that prepared me for a national terror crisis, sleazy bosses, long hours, draining work, and feelings of deep isolation. I had a plan, but I needed to abandon it.

An open mind allows you to see possibilities you didn't

know existed. My experience on the ambassador board clued me in to a new career field; I followed my curiosity, and an exciting path unfolded. An open heart allows you to cultivate resilience and recover when you face disappointment. College will present its share of disappointments and frustrations, whether it's heartbreak over a relationship, your first failing grade, or a deep feeling of homesickness. Don't close those feelings away; give them air and sunlight. You have permission to express *all* of your feelings; only by being truly vulnerable and authentic will you connect with the people who can meet you where you are and help you move forward.

When have you allowed yourself to be surprised? Is there a time you made up your mind about something, only to discover—happily—that you were wrong? Perhaps you thought the new girl at school was snobby, but then you got to know her, and now you've been BFFs since sixth grade. Maybe a friend encouraged you to try a new hobby, and you discovered a passion. Maybe you went through a tough time and your crew abandoned you—yet support and friendship came from the most unlikely places.

We can't plan for everything in life: that's what makes it exciting. As former secretary of state Condoleezza Rice said: "Life is full of surprises and serendipity. Being open to unexpected turns in the road is an important part of success."

In this chapter, we'll meet trailblazers who were heading down one road when their curiosity was sparked by another. The way wasn't clear; they couldn't shine a flashlight down the path and see their one-year, five-year, and ten-year benchmarks. These influencers sometimes could not even see the next step; yet they leaned into the support offered by those around them and forged ahead anyway. They learned a lesson we can all benefit from: less thinking, more feeling. Your rational mind can only get you so far, while your intuition can carry you to places you never dreamed of.

. . . .

Joshua Habermann: One Moment That Changed Everything

Joshua Habermann is a choral music conductor who has conducted groups all over the world. Today, he is director of the Santa Fe Desert Chorale and the Dallas Symphony Chorus. Joshua has served on the faculties of San Francisco State University, Frost School of Music at the University of Miami, and the University of North Texas.

Joshua has the type of career in music that others only dream of—yet becoming a professional musician was never his plan. From an early age, Joshua had a deep love of languages; he thought he would become a translator. Joshua studied abroad in Chile during high school and then spent his freshman year abroad in Sweden; he focused on language acquisition in both locales. According to Joshua, his idea of a fun Friday night in high school was to spend time with his Swedish grammar books! Learning languages was not a hobby with a clear return on investment; yet Joshua loved it, so he persisted.

After his year abroad, Joshua was faced with the decision of where to study for the remainder of undergrad. He applied to several elite schools and got accepted to all of them—which was a marked difference from when he'd applied in high school and been accepted to *none* of these same universities! (Joshua saw the situation clearly; he was suddenly more attractive to colleges because he'd spent his freshman year abroad. Which brings me back to the message of chapter nine—rejection is not personal, is often arbitrary, and doesn't have to be the final word.) Joshua eventually settled on Georgetown and enrolled as a Spanish major.

Joshua had always enjoyed music as a hobby. He joined Georgetown's choir and played the piano but did not think of pursuing music as a major. He *couldn't*—Georgetown didn't have a music degree. Yet Joshua's teachers kept asking him to assist in various capacities, such as playing piano for mass and the school musical. According to Joshua, if he'd gone to a school with a "legit" music program, he never would have had a chance to step into these leadership roles. Yet even though Joshua's talents didn't "measure up" to his perceived standards, he was told by his conductors: "You're the best we've got." The thought ran through the back of Joshua's mind: "Does anyone know I'm not qualified?"

The turning point for Joshua came when he was on the verge of quitting choir. He thought he was involved in too many things and was planning to let music go. Joshua's teacher wanted him to stay; after all, Joshua was a leader in the group. Joshua's teacher decided to make his leadership official; she asked Joshua to conduct the choir.

This appealed to Joshua, who had always enjoyed teaching. He stuck with choir. Then one day not long after, Joshua was pedaling his bicycle through a cold East Coast winter day. He was listening to his Walkman (a precursor to the iPod!) and was transported by the music he heard. The classical music of Strauss calmed Joshua's mind, and a new thought began to emerge: *This is it.*

Joshua began to see that music was what he wanted to do with the rest of his life. "It wasn't something I could name or put my finger on," said Joshua, "except to say that, this music thing is so much bigger than I realized." Joshua got a hint of his future career, yet the path was anything but clear. He was three and a half years into his Spanish degree; changing majors was off the table. (Besides—Georgetown had no music program!) Joshua approached his music teachers and said he would finish his Spanish degree, but he wanted to pursue music as a career.

Joshua's teachers were thrilled that he wanted to lean into his gifts and pursue music. He began meeting with them privately in small tutoring sessions for which he paid $20 an hour, and they filled him in on the remainder of what amounted to a music degree. From there, Joshua took a few gap years—in Thailand teaching Spanish, then in his hometown of San Francisco. In San Francisco, Joshua became heavily involved in choir and a cappella groups again. He was told about an exciting conductor working out of University of Texas at Austin and traveled to meet him. Joshua was super impressed; he and the conductor figured out a way for Joshua to travel to Austin on scholarship and go to grad school in the conductor's new program. The rest is history.

LESSONS FROM JOSHUA'S STORY

- **Pursue things just because you're interested in them.** When Joshua was a high school and undergrad student studying languages, he couldn't have known that he was preparing for his eventual career as a world-renowned choral conductor. Yet a firm grasp of languages is a skill of key importance for the vocal arts, given the vast repertoire of works in German, French, Italian, Spanish, Russian ... understanding the language is key to understanding the music. Joshua liked languages, so he studied them. Period. He had vague thoughts of a future career, but Joshua learned languages for the fun of it.

- **Do you have "just for the fun of it" hobbies?** Often, we hold ourselves back from pursuing our curiosity because we don't see how a certain activity will fit into our life plan. Yet there's an invisible thread that runs through our lives and connects one thing to everything else. We can't see the whole tapestry, how the development of one skill leads to success in a completely unrelated field. Some hobbies are just for joy—and that's wonderful, too. Pursue your interests *now*; you'll have fun, and you never know where they may lead.

- **Impostor syndrome is a liar.** Have you ever heard of the term "impostor syndrome?" It's the belief that you're unqualified—that at any moment, someone will see through you and pull the plug on your dreams. Joshua dealt with it. He wasn't pursuing a "real" music

degree and surely lacked the talent of people studying formally. (Or so he thought.) Yet Joshua's teachers
continued to urge him on toward musical leadership.
They saw his skills clearly, despite all the reasons
Joshua had created in his mind about why he wasn't
qualified to lead. Clearly, Joshua's teachers were right;
he went on to get a master's and a doctorate in music
and now leads choirs all over the world.

- **If a mentor or teacher sees your gifts, suspend
  your disbelief.** Others are often able to see clearly
  what we are unable to see in ourselves. Let the confi-
  dence of trusted mentors be louder than the voice of
  impostor syndrome.

- **Personal relationships and ingenuity count for more
  than a college degree.** When Joshua was nearing the
  end of his undergrad degree and realized he wanted to
  switch course, he leveraged his relationships to help him
  fill in his missing skill set. For $20 an hour, Joshua essen-
  tially got a second degree! (Google current tuition rates
  per hour at your top-choice college—$20 an hour is the
  steal of all steals.) Joshua and his teachers ingeniously
  cobbled together a music degree in spare pockets of time.

  Joshua could have done things the traditional
  way—start from zero and get a second bachelor's at
  a different university. Yet Joshua utilized the network
  he had built at Georgetown and made it work. He
  had the skills, even though he didn't have the music
  degree to prove it. Joshua continued his education
  via private lessons when he was back in San Francis-

co—he was fully committed to pursuing music and threw himself into learning. This unofficial education was good enough for Joshua to be accepted to grad school (with a scholarship!) in an exciting program.

- **The lesson:** you have so many more assets than you realize. There are people in your life who will *jump* at the chance to help you, just as Joshua's teachers did for him. If you're at point A and point B seems a million miles away, yet you're determined to get there . . . get scrappy! Use your imagination and your network. There may be less distance to travel than you realize.

Think you might go into music as a profession someday, or maybe even produce a movie? For an incredible story of the prolific *Pitch Perfect* producer, Deke Sharon, visit www .getrealandgetin.com.

. . . .

Jon Youshaei: A Lucky Encounter With a College Tour Guide

Jon Youshaei grew up a first-generation American, his parents having immigrated from Iran during the revolution. After graduating from college, his father built a successful business selling Oriental rugs. Jon said that even though his family immigrated and was unfamiliar with most aspects of American culture, they had heard of the school Jon would eventually attend: Wharton, the business school at the University of Pennsylvania. A dream school for many of my students, both from the United States and abroad!

Although Wharton was Jon's dream school, he said he had little hope of actually getting in. However, Jon was surrounded by a group of high-achieving peers who encouraged him to go for it anyway. Says Jon: "I really believe in that saying that you're the sum of the people you spend the most time with." Jon's peer group was focused on elite colleges; Jon focused on this goal, too. He worked hard on his application, and was hopeful despite the low probability of acceptance.

One day Jon and his father were on a tour of Penn's campus. They were assigned to one tour guide, yet Jon's father was captivated by another. Jon's dad suggested they switch groups and go with the guide who seemed so confident. "That guy really knows what he's talking about," said Jon's dad.

"But they're tour guides—they *all* know what they're talking about!" Jon was convinced he and his father would get in trouble for switching groups. But they made the switch anyway—thus, Jon was introduced to someone who would become incredibly influential in his life: J.J. Fliegelman.

J.J. told Jon about the Huntsman Program, in which students could gain a liberal arts and business degree at the same time. This is exactly what Jon wanted to do. Jon was an eager listener and asked lots of questions, and J.J. was happy to give advice. He even accompanied Jon and his father to a campus restaurant after the tour and continued to share his knowledge. During the application process, Jon submitted his essays to J.J., who offered feedback. Says Jon, marveling at the experience: "This guy that I met for one afternoon took me under his wing." That was a sign that Jon had found the place he would call home for the next four years.

J.J. continued to be an important mentor to Jon well after Jon gained acceptance to Penn. Jon joined J.J.'s fraternity. J.J. helped Jon navigate the career landscape; after college, J.J. helped Jon weigh his early career options. Today, Jon is recognized as a top marketer who, according to *Inc.* magazine, has "cracked the code for going viral." In addition to being a marketing guru, Jon is a business writer, cartoonist, and speaker. In fact, NPR named a speech Jon delivered as one of "The Best Commencement Speeches, Ever," alongside speeches from luminaries such as JFK, Steve Jobs, and Sheryl Sandberg.[1]

Had Jon's father not followed his hunch, Jon may have had a very different trajectory. This is so often the way life works; we have a chance encounter with someone and a gut feeling. In these moments of fate, lifelong relationships that alter the course of our destinies are born.

LESSONS FROM JON'S STORY

- **Surround yourself with dreamers.** Jon didn't see Wharton as a possibility for himself—yet the people closest to him believed in the dream. Jon leaned on their belief and went for it, despite his doubts. Jon reflected on this, and the maxim that's often trotted out to explain why you need to surround yourself with people who will help you reach higher: "You're the sum of the people you spend the most time with."

- **Who is in your inner circle?** Who do you interact with most on a daily basis? Find a crew that will inspire you to go beyond what you think is possible. Here's another quote: "Great minds discuss ideas; average minds discuss events; small minds discuss people." Are you surrounded by cattiness and gossip? Are you afraid to walk away from your "friends," because you know they'll talk behind your back? If so, time to find a new group of people who believe in you. If you can't find them where you are, seek them out elsewhere.

- **College is the perfect time to consider what you really want in friendships and build relationships with high-vibe people.** Don't worry about ditching long-lasting relationships or about what you "owe" to the people you've known the longest. (Maybe the problem isn't friends; maybe you need to cut ties with a certain family member who always brings you down. That's okay—this journey is about *you*, not about how others may perceive or judge you.) The sooner you hook up with a crew of kind, ambitious people, the more set up for success you'll be. Find people who can hold the vision for you and believe in your potential even when your own belief wavers.

- **It's okay to break rules that don't actually matter.** When Jon's dad suggested they switch tour groups, Jon was scared they were breaking some kind of rule. He was in the "rule-follower" mindset that can serve you well in high school—after all, in high school there *are* lots of rules that need to be followed. Yet Jon's father knew something that comes with age and experience: it's okay to break rules that don't actually matter. No one was harmed by Jon and his father switching groups—and because they did, Jon met someone who would change the course of his life.

- **In college, there won't be people looking over your shoulder like there are in high school.** You can skip class or go, engage in Greek life or not, stay up till 3 a.m. every night playing video games or get a full eight hours of sleep. (I don't advise giving in to the video-game-zombie lifestyle, but it's an option.) The most important thing to remember is that *you have power.* Find yourself in a miserable roommate situation? Ask for a change! Break into a nervous sweat each day as you head for class? Switch majors! Didn't get into a class you've got your heart set on? Appeal!

- **Break out of the high school mindset.** There is not an invisible set of rules governing your behavior—you *make* the rules. That's what being an adult is all about.

- **Long shots aren't as long as you think.** There's a great quote from Bob Iger, who served as Disney's CEO for 15 years. In Bob's tenure as CEO, he oversaw some *major* deals: the acquisition of Pixar, Marvel, Lucasfilm, and Fox. That's why you can stream all the Marvel and Star Wars movies on Disney+, another product that rolled out during Iger's leadership. Under Bob Iger, Disney took over the world— yet each acquisition was incredibly risky. None was a "given"; Iger had to aggressively sell Disney board members on each idea. Here's what Iger says about taking "big swings" in his book, *The Ride of a Lifetime* (emphasis mine):

People sometimes shy away from taking big swings because they assess the odds and build a case against trying something before they even take the first step. One of the things I've always instinctively felt . . . is that long shots aren't usually as long as they seem.

This was certainly true for Jon. He thought Wharton was impossible—then he got in. Later, Jon was voted class president. Even more notably, Jon was awarded the Spoon Award upon graduation. The Spoon Award has been given to students for nearly 150 years; Jon Huntsman, for whom the Huntsman Program in International Studies and Business is named, received the award himself. The award is decided by peer vote; Jon's classmates chose him as a leader on campus. Said Jon: "I went from not thinking I would ever get into Penn to getting into Penn, getting elected class president, and then winning this historic award. It was just mind boggling to a family that didn't have any roots in America a generation before, and here we are on an Ivy League campus."

Jon had traveled an incredibly vast distance in four short years. Today, Jon is a long way away from the high school kid who thought he had no shot at admission. That's how our big dreams are. They seem impossible: then one day they're not. Soon after, we're looking at our "impossible" dreams in the rearview mirror as we drive toward the next big adventure. Jon's long shot wasn't so long—and neither is yours.

REFLECTION QUESTIONS

Joshua Habermann and Jon Youshaei both experienced an unexpected moment of fate that changed everything. We can't plan for these serendipities—yet we can seize them when they appear. Your intuition—not your rational mind—is your guide. Grab your journal and reflect on these questions:

1. Have you ever had a magical moment when you realized a certain thing was "meant to be"? Perhaps a person who became an instant best friend, a sudden realization of an action you needed to take, a strong desire to go to a particular place, etc.
2. How did you recognize this moment? Reflect on what it *felt* like (tingly feeling in your fingers, expansiveness in your chest, etc.).
3. Joshua's calling to pursue music didn't "make sense," as Georgetown didn't have a music degree. Jon's father's intuition required he and Jon to break the rules and switch tour groups, which Jon was reluctant to do. Did your rational mind try to dissuade you from following your intuition?
4. What was the payoff for following your intuition?

An open heart will lead you to success faster than thinking your way there ever could. What's more: when you stay open to the people, possibilities, and magic life has to offer, you'll *enjoy* each part of your journey. Remember: try not to sweat the small stuff. Don't keep your nose to the grindstone *all* the time—instead, look up and look around. You never know what magic you'll find just around the corner.

TWELVE

Chart Your Own Path

*Do not go where the path may lead, go instead
where there is no path and leave a trail.*

—RALPH WALDO EMERSON

Once upon a time there was a girl named E. E had a secret she
was determined to keep locked inside. She was *sure* that once
the world learned her secret, she would be shunned—so E
shunned herself. She hid away from people to protect herself
and her secret. The price she paid was huge—but as long as
the truth of herself was hidden away, E was "safe," and so was
everyone around her.

But one day, to E's horror, her secret came bursting forth. E
was certain that unleashing her secret had caused irreparable
harm and that the one person she loved would now turn her
back on her. And so E broke the rules and escaped the only
life she had known—a life full of rules she did not create but
was forced to uphold. E escaped a life of lies in search of her
deepest truth. She charted her own path—and in so doing,
wondered at all the time she had spent living from someone

else's playbook. E was done with that. In E's own words: "It's time to see what I can do, to test the limits and break through."

Okay . . . so E is not an actual person, but Elsa from the movie *Frozen*. (Remember: I have a young child! Elsa is *very real* in my house.) Real or animated, Elsa's story is a beautiful illustration of what it looks like to begin living from your own truth.

Remember the part in "Let It Go" where Elsa is flying up the icy staircase, creating each step with her power as she goes? It's exhilarating. It almost seems as if Elsa will outrun her powers—like she'll fly off the stairs and plummet down the mountain before her magic can create the next place for her foot to land. Yet we trust the exuberant smile on Elsa's face. She is safe because she is free. If Elsa were to fall, she would simply use her magic to catch herself. There is nothing Elsa needs that is outside of herself.

As you chart your path toward success, you'll have countless chances to test your powers and see what you're made of. Perhaps you'll choose a traditional job with clearly marked benchmarks and milestones. For instance, if you want to become a doctor, the way is clear: college, medical school, residency, practice. Yet even in this "traditional" path, creativity and ingenuity are required. Where will you go to medical school? How will you balance the demands of school and then residency with your other responsibilities? Which field of medicine will you enter? Will an additional fellowship be required? No two careers in medicine are exactly alike, even if the steps that led to those careers were equivalent.

You may feel called to chart a completely unknown

path—to, like Elsa, leap before the landing appears. The truth is, *you can't know* how your path will look. Just like Joshua and Jon experienced unexpected twists of fate they couldn't possibly have foreseen, you can't plan for these things. Often, people who've successfully charted their own course did so because they were pursuing other, more traditional career paths—and hated it. They *had* to make their own way, because the course they were on was so deeply unsatisfying. In *Leaves of Grass*, Walt Whitman tells us to "re-examine all you have been told in school or church or in any book, and dismiss whatever insults your soul."

In this chapter, we'll meet Ezina LeBlanc and Thomas Kail. Ezina is a former Miss Black USA; after college, she found herself on a career trajectory charted by her parents. So Ezina stepped off the known path and began the creation of a wholly unique, multi-varied, and successful career. How did she do it? Just like Elsa—one step at a time. We'll also meet Thomas Kail, the award-winning director of none other than *Hamilton*, one of the most celebrated musical theater works of all time. Thomas followed his curiosity and blazed his own trail to dizzying heights. Ready to see how they did it—and how you can, too?

Read on.

Ezina LeBlanc: Blazing Her Own Trail

Ezina LeBlanc grew up in a household rich with culture and tradition. Ezina's mother is Jewish and Native American; her father is Native American and Caribbean. Ezina's parents and grandparents were ambitious and committed to helping their community; from a young age, Ezina was encouraged to learn and help those who were less fortunate. Ezina said that her family was not one to sit around and watch TV; rather, they frequently volunteered at soup kitchens and helped local charities. Ezina's household ethos revolved around *tikkun olam*, a Hebrew phrase that means "repair the world."

Ezina had a great relationship with her family; today, she appreciates the values they instilled in her. Yet this did not mean that Ezina saw eye to eye with her parents growing up. Ezina was a musician and had her heart set on attending Juilliard; Ezina's parents said this was out of the question. Her second choice was Pepperdine—but Ezina's parents shot down that option, too. The school they wanted Ezina to attend was where she eventually ended up: the University of Michigan.

At Michigan, Ezina got a bachelor's in business and then an MBA. Her parents wanted her to be a lawyer, so after business school Ezina attended law school—for one year. "Enough was enough," said Ezina. "I felt like I was just checking off boxes for my parents."

Rather than complete law school, Ezina switched course and made good on the dream she'd had before undergrad: attending Juilliard. According to Ezina, this move was hard for her parents to understand; her mother thought Ezina should finish what she had started. Yet Ezina had zero interest in the law, although her parents and grandparents encouraged her in that direction. Ezina's business degrees also confused her parents. According to Ezina, there were two "respectable" paths for her to take: law and medicine. An MBA didn't fit into either of those categories, and her parents didn't understand how she would earn a living with the degree.

Yet receiving her MBA was actually the perfect training for Ezina's eventual career as an artist (more on that in a moment). Ezina applied to Juilliard—a highly prestigious school many parents would be thrilled for their child to attend—feeling like she was the "worst kid ever" for not finishing law school. Ezina was accepted; she studied opera to realize her dream of becoming a professional opera singer. Yet this was the 1990s; there were even fewer opera singers of color than today. Ezina would go on audition after audition, only to be told that the starring role was meant to be "Italian or German"— white. "But we can put you in the chorus," the casting directors would say. Ezina reflected on her thoughts at the time: "I didn't sign up to be in the chorus the rest of my life."

Fast forward to today. Ezina is now an independent artist who owns her own record label. She performs concerts all over the world—in every concert, she sings an operatic aria. Ezina said that her performances of these arias catch her audience by surprise since her recorded music is more in the world music genre.

The more Ezina began to travel giving concerts, the more people asked her questions. They wanted to know how she could afford to tour, how she'd created a sustainable lifestyle for herself without being a household name. To answer their questions, Ezina began writing books (to date, she's written 20!). Yet Ezina realized that the people asking her questions needed even more support and guidance, so she began creating courses and learning experiences through which artists could learn how to make money. Here is where Ezina's business background kicked in; she used her entrepreneurial smarts to create financial success for herself and has helped countless other artists do the same. Said Ezina: "Artists make life livable . . . I don't believe in starving artists. There's so many ways for [artists] to make money."

Ezina's background in business prepared her for a career as a musician. This is completely contrary to what students are taught in music school—there, the focus is entirely on getting better at your instrument in the hopes of one day receiving an appointment in a professional music ensemble. Musicians aren't taught to make their own way—yet Ezina did. Ezina has put her unique skill set to work and crafted a life and career that seems impossible to outsiders. Each day, she teaches others how to live the impossible.

LESSONS FROM EZINA'S STORY

- **Your choices need to make sense to *you*—not anyone else.** Ezina's parents were confused by her choice to go to business school and then to complete her MBA. Yet to Ezina, it was the most exciting path available at the time. It takes courage to stand for the choices you've made, especially when everyone around you questions them. Even for seemingly insignificant choices—like which extracurricular activities to pursue, how often you should come home from college, whether or not to dye your hair—make the choice that feels best to *you*. Perhaps you have loved ones who like to weigh in on every decision in your life. Do you find yourself "going along with the flow?" There's a price to pay for always agreeing to someone else's decisions—even if you love the person or the person insists that the decision they've made *for* you is in your best interest.

- **Check in with yourself regularly.** The major you're considering—whose idea was it? Are you constantly justifying your actions to yourself? This sounds like: "I'll do this for one year, and then I can do something else." Or, "I owe it to myself to try this thing, since Dad always said I'd be good at it." Hear this: *you owe yourself happiness.* If you're living out someone else's choices, you can fake happiness for a while—but it won't last. Don't worry if your loved ones aren't on board with your choices: just stand firm in your truth and let other people either fall away or come along with you.

- **You don't have to finish everything you start.** Even though Ezina felt like the "worst kid ever" for not completing law school, she made the right decision by dropping out. Staying in law school would have meant two more years of an expensive degree that she had no intention of translating into a career—and the time cost would have been even more expensive than the dollar value. Ezina had already given one year of her life to the pursuit of something that brought her no joy. In her own words, "Enough was enough." Up until now, you've not had much choice about whether or not to follow through on your commitments. You *have* to finish high school in order to attend college; when you're under your parents' roof, you pretty much have to do what they say. Things become a lot scarier (and more exciting!) when you get to decide which commitments to keep. Continue to break out of the high school mindset, which we discussed in the last chapter. If something is making you miserable, *don't do it.* With time, you'll get better at discerning which responsibilities to pursue. In the meantime, let go of the things that bring you down. You don't need 'em.

- **Treat yourself like a business.** There's a reason the stereotype of the "starving artist" exists in our culture. We have the expectation that, if you want to make money, you enter professions such as business, law, or medicine. Not too many people think, "I'll be a stage actress and make bank!" or "I'll follow my passion in textile arts and the money will just roll in!" Ezina said that our society is accustomed to underpaying the artist. While we would never ask someone to fill our cavities or cut our hair for free, we profit from the unpaid work of artists all the time. Ezina thinks this is wrong, since "artists make life livable."
- **In Ezina's words:** "You have to treat yourself like a business." Ezina leaned on her business undergrad and graduate degrees as she crafted a profitable life as an artist. She was doing email marketing back in 1995—long before most people had email! Ezina

said that almost half of the people who began following her in the midnineties are still with her. Ezina built a committed fan base that she has nurtured and grown. When artists come to Ezina saying they can't make money, Ezina breaks down their businesses with them to see where they're leaving money on the table. It's not all about the money, or about seeing how you can milk people for dollar bills. What a financially secure career in the arts *is* about is ensuring you have your needs met so that you are free to explore creatively and create work that is meaningful and beautiful. That's hard to do if you're wondering how you'll afford groceries!

- As Ezina has proven, a career in the arts doesn't have to equal a life of financial hardship. Treating yourself like a business allows you to think strategically and see what needs to be done. No matter if you work for yourself or for someone else; if you treat yourself like a business, you'll ensure you're making the best decisions for your financial future. That security will enable you to think outside the box and flourish.

Thomas Kail: Following His Curiosity to a Brilliant Career

You probably know who Thomas Kail is, even if you don't realize it. Ever binge-listened to the entire cast album of *Hamilton* . . . and then listened again? Thomas Kail is Lin-Manuel Miranda's collaborator and the director of

Hamilton. He also collaborated with Miranda and directed *In the Heights*, the smash hit musical that won four Tony Awards and is now a movie. I was fortunate to interview him in *Forbes* about the Hamilton Prize for Creativity, which is an award that he and Miranda underwrote to support a student's creativity.[1]

Thomas Kail has tasted the type of blockbuster success that only comes around once a decade or so. Yet musical theater and directing were not on Thomas's radar when he entered Wesleyan University. Thomas had grown up playing soccer at a high level; he thought he would become a sportscaster and began college with that intention. However, Thomas was asked to assist on a student stage production his junior year. That experience changed everything. Said Thomas: "I was looking for a team and stumbled into theater."

When Thomas began his career in theater, he started as an assistant stage manager. This meant he was responsible for jobs many would view as menial, such as sweeping the stage. Yet Thomas approached each task and each job with a high level of responsibility. Said Thomas: "I had to sweep the stage in the most efficient, best way possible, because that's what my job was." Thomas said that whatever job he had he treated as if it were the most important thing in the world—whether he was driving a van to pick up actors or directing the cast of *Hamilton* on opening night.

Thomas didn't set out to have a career in theater, yet he followed his curiosity and charted his own course to his current success. He spoke of the importance of a "beginner's mind." "Beginner's mind" is a Buddhist term; it means a state of openness, a lack of judgment about the people or circumstances around you. Said Thomas: "I just kept meeting people who surprised me." The people he met encouraged Thomas in the theater path he had begun to pursue. After college, Thomas continued to place himself in situations where he could be surprised by and learn from others. These traits of openness and curiosity have a direct correlation with Thomas's success as a director, where his main job is to draw out others and empower them to do their jobs on and off the stage.

LESSONS FROM THOMAS'S STORY

- **No one achieves success solo.** Whether or not you knew Thomas Kail's work before reading this chapter, you've probably been impacted by his work. (I can't think of anyone who doesn't know *Hamilton*!) I'd wager that you *have* heard of Lin-Manuel Miranda. While Miranda is a household name, he couldn't have created the cultural phenomenon that is *Hamilton* without Thomas Kail. Their collaboration, begun in 2002, has quickly become one of the most important in Broadway history.
- Likewise, Thomas would not be where he is today without Lin-Manuel Miranda. There's a line in *Hamilton* that holds significance for both Lin-Manuel and Thomas: "The world was wide enough for both Hamilton and me."[2] The line is about how another's success doesn't preclude your own. In fact, the success of collaborators and peers actually *increases* your chance of success. There's a saying that "a rising

tide lifts all ships." Rather than becoming jealous of peers' successes, take a page from Thomas's book and lean into relationships.

- Thomas's gift for relationships is what enables his success as a director. Thomas said that as he works with each individual involved in a production, he communicates with them in a way that will allow them to do their best work. That means Thomas frequently has to change his style of communication, or code-switch. Thomas is willing to be flexible and adaptable because he knows that that approach yields the best result. Each success he's experienced has been the product of a mighty team effort. How can you honor the relationships in your life and lean into them? Remember the African proverb: "If you want to go fast, go alone. If you want to go far, go together." Your success will not be of your own making, no matter how much people like to claim that they're "self-made." Success is always a team sport.

- **Treat each job you have like it's the most important job on earth**. When Thomas began his career in theater, he was starting from zero. Some people might have viewed sweeping stages or driving vans as beneath them. Yet to Thomas, the duties were vitally important. Imagine if he hadn't done his job well and an actor had tripped over a stray electrical cord and broken an ankle. Such a scenario would put the whole production in a bind. Thomas rightly knew the importance of so-called menial tasks, and he gave them his all.

- You may graduate college hungry for glory. The ladder between entry-level role and VIP can seem impossibly steep—and there are no guarantees when you'll climb each rung. This is a tough transition! High school is four years, college is four years—but what's the timeline on becoming successful given your own definition of what success should look like? The truth is that there is no specific timeline. That uncertainty can breed impatience. Often, newer workers see the job they *want* far off in the distance—thus, they give a half-effort to the job they *have* because they're dreaming of something better. Yet the surest way to advance—personally and professionally—is to give your all to whatever's right in front of you. Remember: in every work situation, there is something to be learned. You most likely won't land in your dream job right away, but you can learn from mentors and gain every valuable skill that workplace has to offer. Wherever you are, strive for excellence. It's the quickest way to get to what's next.

- **Leadership means empowering others to be their best.** Thomas knew the importance of a strong team long before his theater days—he learned about team dynamics on the high school soccer field. Whether or not he was the most "important" person on the field, Thomas always knew how important his job was: seeing the whole game, identifying strengths in his teammates, and bringing those strengths to the fore. He knew that, in every practice, he could empower the other players to be their best. As a director, Thomas's job is the same: hire the best people, empower them, and then get out of their way so they can perform their own brand of magic.

- This is what it means to be a leader. Who's on your "team"? You may play a sport and have literal teammates. Or maybe you're a section leader in band; maybe you're organizing a fundraiser or event and are responsible for delegating duties. Wherever you're called to step into the role of leader—now, in college, or when you enter the workforce—step into that role by working as hard as you can and bringing out the best in others. As we've discussed, extraordinary success often requires collaboration and the efforts of many individuals. Some people say that if your dream for your life doesn't involve a team, you're not dreaming big enough. Whether or not you *feel* like a leader, begin to try on that identity. Whether or not you realize it, others are looking to you—even if it's just your little cousin or the kids you babysit down the street. Acknowledge that you *are* a leader, think of who's on your team, and look for ways to lift them.

REFLECTION QUESTIONS

The stories of Ezina and Thomas highlight an interesting paradox: to chart your own course, you need others. None of us exists in a vacuum; every decision we make impacts those around us. To blaze your own trail, you may first need to buck the well-meaning advice of parents and mentors and follow your passion, as Ezina did. But Ezina hasn't achieved her success as a solo act—even if she's billed that way in a concert. She's had collaborators and band members and business partners for nearly three decades. Ezina struck out on her own, then found a team.

Likewise, collaboration has been a key ingredient in Thomas's success at each point in his journey. His role as a director is similar to that of an entrepreneur: each production is a startup in which the personnel must come together quickly, form close relationships, and deliver a memorable product. As the leader, Thomas is responsible for setting the tone and leading the group to the finish line. He doesn't lead by barking orders and demanding greatness; instead, he meets each individual where they are and nurtures what's best in them so they can be even better.

Consider these questions—you may want to jot down your answers in a journal:

1. Have you ever created something from nothing, as Ezina created her music career and personal brand?
2. Do you believe that "the world is wide enough" for you and your peers, or do you feel a sense of scarcity and competition? If so, how could you reframe your thinking and prize collaboration over competition?
3. Do you have any role models who've charted a wholly original course to success? What have you learned

from them? Could you nurture those relationships and
learn even more?

You have everything you need to succeed. Trying to follow
someone else's path is a losing game—you'll *never* be able to,
because you can't *be* anyone else. In the immortal words of Dr.
Seuss: "You have brains in your head. You have feet in your
shoes. You can steer yourself in any direction you choose."

My advice: make sure you're headed somewhere fun.

THIRTEEN

Turn Lemons Into Lemonade

*Life is what happens to us while
we are making other plans.*
—ALLEN SAUNDERS

In life, anything can happen. We can't plan for serendipities like the ones Joshua Habermann and Jon Youshaei experienced when they discovered their future career paths and business partners in moments of fate. Likewise, we can't plan for tragedy. Bumps in the road catch us by surprise—sometimes, in an instant, the entire world is turned upside down.

No one could have known that, mere weeks after I began college at NYU, New York City would be ground zero for the worst-ever terrorist attack on U.S. soil. In the days, weeks, and months following 9/11, the world changed dramatically. Planes stopped flying. New threats emerged left and right— the threat of another terrorist attack, the question of impending war, fear over anthrax poisoning (anthrax is a spore that causes a serious bacterial disease; immediately after 9/11, several packages containing anthrax spores were mailed to news outlets and U.S. senators in an act of bioterrorism). Life as we knew it in the United States ceased to exist; no one knew what would emerge from the wreckage of 9/11.

As I write this, the world is in the grips of the coronavirus pandemic. Life has again ground to a halt. Perhaps you were forced to finish your high school career from home and missed out on key rites of passage like graduation and the senior trip you'd been looking forward to for years. Colleges have had to overhaul their admission requirements and implement new systems for every operation they perform. In the relatively short period of time since quarantines were enacted in March 2020, some colleges have gone bankrupt. While we in the United States caught glimpses of the severity of the pandemic via news outlets that covered the crisis in China, and then in Europe, no one was prepared for how quickly the crisis reached the United States and how fast life changed. Large-scale crises are like that. Experts can plan for them and try their best to prepare; yet when the crisis hits, there is always an element of surprise and confusion. Though we can do our best to prepare for hard times, we can't *know* what it's like to be in a difficult situation until we're in it.

You've probably heard the expression "when life hands you a lemon, make lemonade." The expression refers to your ability to perform alchemy. Alchemy was the medieval forerunner to chemistry; alchemists strove to turn ordinary matter into gold. When the universe hands you something sour (like a lemon), how can you transform it into something sweet? When you're given dirt, how do you make it gold?

Note: not all lemons look the same! For one person, a lemon

may be their experience of being bullied in middle school. Someone else's lemon may be their parents' divorce. Whether you're dealing with the death of a loved one, a traumatic family move, childhood abuse, a home life steeped in poverty and deprivation, or anxiety and depression—whatever you're going through is *yours*. We're not in the business of comparing lemons. Rather, let's acknowledge that whatever you're facing is real; your lemon is plenty sour, whatever its shape. Yet even the most lumpy, sour lemon can make a delicious lemonade.

In this chapter, we'll meet individuals who endured times that pushed them to their limits in every conceivable way. These individuals kept their hearts open; they cultivated resilience, even in the darkest times, by sharing their struggles. From these struggles, beautiful things were born. These alchemists turned their suffering into gold; you can do the same.

. . . .

Laura Orrico: From Devastating Tragedy, a New Career Is Born

Laura Orrico is a film and television actress whose comedic chops have landed her guest spots on shows like *That '70s Show*, *The King of Queens*, and *Kevin Can Wait*. Laura is from the Midwest; she attended Columbia College in Chicago, where she received her bachelor's in television writing and producing with a minor in acting. Laura grew up idolizing comedic greats like Lucille Ball and Gilda Radner. After college, she began attending classes and eventually performing with the famed Second City theater troupe in Chicago. (Famous alumni of Second City include Tina Fey, Steve Carell of *The*

Office, and Bill Murray.) Laura got experience both behind the camera—writing and producing for a TV show based out of Chicago—and in front of the camera (her big break came when she landed a shampoo commercial!).

Yet life threw Laura a major curveball. In 2015, Laura's husband, Ryan, passed away after a long cancer battle. During the last year of her husband's life, Laura stepped back from her acting career and served as his full-time caregiver. Mixed in with the emotional strain of caring for her dying husband was the fear of what came next. Laura knew she would have to figure out a way to support herself. Said Laura: "That was a fear of mine . . . not knowing if I'd be able to survive on my own."

Nearly a year after her husband passed away, a friend reached out to Laura asking for help with public relations. From that request, Laura's new business was born. Laura had been doing PR for herself for most of her career. Following her friend's request, Laura decided to leverage those skills and do for other people the PR work she *wished* she'd been able to hire someone to do for her. Said Laura: "Connecting people, networking on my clients' behalf, and helping them get notoriety . . . it just comes easy, and it's fun."

When Laura started her new business, she didn't give up her first love of acting. Laura still pursues acting as a hobby, like other people enjoy tennis or ceramics as hobbies. Laura said that her acting passion is an outlet that's available for her whenever she needs.

LESSONS FROM LAURA'S STORY

- **Follow your path of least resistance.** In what areas are you naturally gifted? What strengths do you have that don't feel like strengths—they just feel like things that are fun and easy for you? Laura enjoyed connecting people and networking. Following those talents led her to the creation of her PR firm.

- **You can build a beautiful career for yourself** by focusing on the things that are easy and fun for you. This is not the message we receive from our culture. We're told to work on making our weaknesses better in the interest of being "well rounded." Yet the people who have built massive success have done it by doubling down on their strengths. This means building a career around the things that are easy and fun— following your path of least resistance. When you get paid for doing things you love, it feels like you're getting away with something. "But this is so *easy* for me . . . should I really get money for it?"

- **Yes, you should!** Because the things that are enjoyable to you are unimaginably difficult for someone else. Maybe you could spend all day designing and setting up websites; yet the very thought of registering for a domain name makes someone else break out in hives. Do you live for public speaking and being in front of a crowd? Other people would sooner jump out of an airplane. Just because something is easy for you doesn't mean you can't be incredibly successful pursuing it. When you work hard doing activities you actually *like*, the work doesn't feel like work; it feels like play.

- **Talk about your lemons.** While Laura's husband was going through his cancer battle, Laura shared her journey on social media. She and Ryan decided they were going to share all the parts of their journey, good and bad. So often, we only see people's "highlight reels" on social media. You hear about when your friend from camp got accepted into college—but not about when her first-choice school sent a rejection, or her second-choice school put her on the wait list. You see your soccer teammate doing a funny dance— but you don't hear about how his parents are in the middle of a messy divorce.

- Laura and Ryan decided to tell the truth. By sharing her journey on Facebook, she was able to receive support from people from every corner of her universe. But not only was she receiving help; Laura was also offering help. After her husband's death, many people approached Laura and shared how her posts had helped them in lots of different ways. Some of Laura's audience had experienced a perspective shift: by seeing Laura and Ryan's struggles, readers realized that their own problems were not as big as they thought. Other readers had loved ones in critical care; Laura's posts gave them tools to better communicate with hospital workers. Because Laura talked about her lemons—the tough stuff—rather than hide them away, she was able to have richer connections with the people in her life.

- "Talk about your lemons" does not mean "post complaints on social media" or "whine to your friends." Talking about your lemons means being real about the things that are hard and being open to help. As Laura learned, help can come from the places you least expect. In turn, you never know whom *you* may be helping by speaking your truth.

- **Always do the things that make you happy.** In the final year of her husband's life, Laura put her acting career on hold to take care of him. Acting is a very uncertain profession, and Laura and Ryan were in a very uncertain time; Laura needed to focus on what was most important. Laura did not know how she was going to support herself when her husband passed; yet a new opportunity presented itself, and Laura began a new career.

- Yet even though acting is no longer Laura's primary way to pay the bills, she still makes time to pursue it. Too often, we think the only activities that "count" are the ones we get paid for (or the ones that count toward our GPA). Yet if we're not making time for the things that make us happy, those other activities can feel empty. We can lose ourselves in activities that hold no meaning for us. Do you love running—but you're not on the cross-country team anymore and you feel that you need to be in labs all day as you work toward your pre-med degree? Break out those sneakers and hit a trail. Do you love to sing but think, "What's the point, I'm not in choir?" Drink some lemon tea, close the door, and belt it out in your bathroom. Getting recognition and money for your hobbies is nice—but the real value in these activities exists in the joy they bring you. Protect your joy at all costs.

None of us is actively seeking out pain and loss. But when we experience these feelings, they can become an inspiration to build something fresh. Visit www.getrealandgetin.com to learn about Clarissa Silva, whose childhood challenges and personal difficulties have led her to become one of the world's most highly recognized relationship experts.

. . . .

Jordan Taylor Wright: Transforming Anxiety and Depression Into a Mindfulness Movement

Jordan Taylor Wright, founder of Taylor Cut Films, is a creative director and filmmaker based out of Los Angeles. Taylor Cut Films is a production company and creative agency specializing in music videos, commercials, and films. Over a ten-year span Taylor Cut Films has worked and created original content for artists such as Usher, Justin Bieber, Jennifer Lopez, and The Chainsmokers. Jordan says that even in high school he was drawn to the medium of visual storytelling with photography. Jordan took a video production course as a freshman; from that point, he realized he wanted to pursue visual storytelling as a career.

Yet even though Jordan felt sure of his direction from a young age, the path was not always smooth. Jordan's parents, who emigrated from South Africa to America, went through a difficult divorce when Jordan was in late elementary school. Jordan saw a therapist at the time. There, he learned the value of being able to express himself and speak his truth; Jordan learned that *he* was not his *thoughts*. It was an early lesson in mindfulness, which is defined as the "state of being conscious or aware of something." To be mindful means that when a thought crosses your mind, you notice it, but you don't identify with it. A mindful person observes positive and negative thoughts like "I'm not smart enough to understand this," or "This is all my fault," or "I'm the best soccer player in school" yet doesn't attach to them.

This early training in mindfulness came in handy when Jordan later suffered with anxiety and depression. Jordan, as a videographer, got to witness the glamorous "rock star" life up close as he would jet around the world doing shoots for the artists he worked with. Even though these stars had every material thing someone could ask for, Jordan observed that outward success doesn't equal inner happiness. What Jordan noticed is that each person longs to express themselves truly and be understood by others; when that is lacking, no amount of glitz or perks will fill the void that exists in the absence of true connection.

Jordan noticed that he experienced anxiety and depression when he would think about the past or project forward into the future. When he was mulling over past mistakes he believed he'd made, Jordan felt depressed. When he was projecting into the future and imagining how his life could go wrong if he *continued* to make those mistakes, Jordan felt anxious. Yet Jordan noticed something: when he was living in the moment, he was happy. He re-discovered the mindfulness lessons he'd learned as a young boy in therapy during his parents' divorce.

Said Jordan: "If you remove the expectation, you open up your reality for an infinite number of possibilities that you couldn't even anticipate if you wanted to." Jordan found a way through his anxiety and depression by staying in the present moment and letting go of thoughts of the future and the past; as a result, he's "happy, pretty much always." Jordan now uses his platform to spread the mindfulness message.

LESSONS FROM JORDAN'S STORY

- **We all have trauma; yet we choose how we let it shape us.** Trauma is defined as a "deeply distressing or disturbing experience." We tend to reserve the word for dramatic traumas, like a sudden death or a car wreck. Yet under the "trauma" umbrella, I would include non-fatal incidents—your parents' divorce, a sudden move, a change in family structure. Jordan experienced the early trauma of his parents' divorce— something that occurs frequently in American house- holds yet is nonetheless disorienting and confusing for children of divorce. On the scale of traumatic events, we may give divorce a low rating. Yet just because something is common doesn't mean that those who experience it aren't profoundly affected. Remember, like we said in the beginning of this chapter—we're not in the business of comparing lemons. We can never judge someone else's experience from the out- side; only the person going through the hardship has the authority to report on what it's like.

- Through counseling, Jordan got the message that his parents' divorce was separate from him. He didn't cause it by being "bad," and he couldn't fix it by being "good." Jordan came to understand himself as something whole and apart from his parents' relationship. Whatever traumas you face, you can learn to view yourself as *whole* in the face of them. The difficult experience can teach you, yet it doesn't have to define you.

- **Build your life from the inside out.** Jordan said that he attributes his success to identifying the things that make him feel good and then building his life around those things. This is the opposite of what many people do—they build their lives around what they think will make them *look* good. Through Jordan's experience jet-setting with top entertainers, he'd learned that the outward trappings of big success did not equal a happy life. What good is a private jet if you're not smiling? Who cares about designer clothes if you don't have friends?

- It's not that private jets and designer clothes are inherently wrong. If those are your money goals, then go for them! But take a lesson from Jordan, who saw early on that *things* don't equal *happiness*. Jim Carrey, actor and comedian, put it this way: "I think everybody should get rich and famous and do everything they ever dreamed of so they can see it's not the answer." By contrast, when you build your life from the inside out and create it from a place of joy, then *joy* is what you get more of—along with money, recognition, and maybe fame. The money, recognition, and fame are nice side perks; the *real* perk is a life that's a constant source of happiness.

- **You are not your thoughts.** Learning how to detach from thoughts is some of the most important work we can do. If we are defined by our thoughts, we'll never ascend to our highest potential. Jordan first learned this non-identification as a young boy in a therapist's office. Though a traumatic event sent him to the therapist, Jordan was able to take the lesson of mindfulness, or observing thoughts, and carry it with him for the rest of his life.

- Identifying with your thoughts is a losing game, because our thoughts change so rapidly. We're up one minute and down the next. Often, thoughts are not original to us; they're programmed into us by the authority figures in our lives. Our thoughts may tell us that we shouldn't aspire too high—if we listen to them too closely, we'll talk ourselves out of our dreams. Or, they may tell us that we're the *best* and can't lose—but what about when the inevitable happens and we *do* fail? This is to say nothing of people who experience mental illness. For instance, if you live with bipolar disorder and experience manic-depressive episodes, you may be accustomed to your thoughts swinging the pendulum—one day your thoughts say you're untouchable, the next your thoughts say you're a loser. Which is the truth?

Neither. You are not your thoughts; you are the observer of your thoughts. Your value is inherent and fixed, no matter what games your mind wants to play on any particular day. Do you have a mindfulness or meditation practice that allows you to separate from your thoughts and re-connect with your own inner goodness? If not, I recommend starting one. Build up your inner resources so that, when you experience difficult periods and your thoughts turn dark, you'll be able to remember that you are *so much more* than your thoughts. You, my friend, are good. Nothing can change that.

High Achievers and Burnout—
Why It's Dangerous

The lesson Jordan learned and now shares with others, "you are not your thoughts," is one that I wish all college students understood. Your thoughts may be tumultuous in college— particularly in your freshman year. You are finding your place in a strange new world; the world of college may be very different from your high school world. This was true for Madison Holleran, the subject of the book *What Made Maddy Run*, which I referenced in chapter nine.

Maddy, a member of the track team at the University of Pennsylvania, struggled to find her identity as a college athlete. In high school, she'd been *the* star; yet in college, Maddy was squarely in the middle of the pack. Academics presented a new challenge as well. In high school, Maddy earned top grades; in college, she struggled adjusting to being graded on a curve and worried she'd fail her classes. Maddy wasn't equipped to deal with the flipped social order that college presented. She questioned whether she should stay at Penn or quit the track team—Maddy ultimately decided to quit track but worried excessively about burdening her teammates. Even though Maddy visited a therapist, there was a gap between what she shared with her confidantes and the burdens she privately carried. Ultimately, her private burdens proved too heavy; Maddy took her own life.

Maddy's mindset is remarkably common for high-achieving students; where Maddy's story differs from others is the drastic, tragic action she took. When high achievers' experience of college doesn't align with their high school experience, these students become unmoored. If your identity rests in being a straight-A student, then what happens when you get your first B? If you take pride in being a star soccer player, how do you react when you're benched freshman year? The stress to "keep up" with your high school self can be unbearable—and the task may be impossible. College is *meant* to challenge you in new ways, and you're meant to forge a *separate* identity from the one you had senior year of high school. Yet many students lack healthy coping mechanisms and keep chasing their high school achievement levels anyway.

The word "burnout" was coined back in 1974 by Herbert Freudenberger in his book *Burnout: The High Cost of High*

Achievement. He defined burnout as the "extinction of motivation or incentive, especially when one's devotion to a cause or relationship fails to produce the desired results."[1] High achievers and perfectionists are at high risk of burnout. Burnout can look like this:

Losing your "spark," growing cynical, and wondering: "What am I doing all this for? It's no use. I may as well stop trying."

Experiencing body pains, like headaches and stomachaches.

Being in a constant state of exhaustion and losing your ability to complete tasks.

Having a "negative thought loop" in your head and not being able to focus or think creatively.

Burnout can make you feel like there's something wrong with *you*—like you *should* be able to cope with college life just fine, but you're not; you must be doing it wrong. Hear this: the only thing "wrong" are your expectations of yourself.

You're not Superman or Wonder Woman! If the transition from high school to college *feels* hard, that's because it *is* hard. Chances are, you're missing your coping mechanisms from high school—the people and places you've relied on as "pick-me-ups" are likely hundreds or thousands of miles away. (Virtual communication is great, but it's not the same!) You may wonder who you can go to for support; it's up to you to create your own network.

According to Elizabeth Grace Saunders, a time management expert, a feeling of isolation can contribute to burnout. If this is you, consider ways you could find your people in college. This may look like attending a meeting for a student organization, participating in campus activities, or simply striking up a conversation with the friendly-looking girl who sits next to you in psych class. Find the people you can be real with—these should be folks who make you feel *better,* not worse. Saunders identifies five more contributors to burnout, as well as how you can manage them:[2]

Your workload is too much. Perhaps you were over-ambitious in taking on credit hours; now you're drowning in homework and find it impossible to maintain your desired GPA. That's okay. Seriously. If you're a straight-A student, here's what I wish for you: that you make your first B as soon as possible. That way, you'll see that it's not the end of the world!

Can you identify what the *most important* class is, in terms of your interest level and future goals? Could you concentrate on that class and let perfectionism go? Working hard toward something meaningful is rewarding; working hard for the sake of "keeping up appearances" and maintaining a perfect GPA is demoralizing. Focus on what matters.

You feel out of control. In college, you have more control over your schedule and life than in high school. Yet it's still possible to feel out of control—and if that's true for you, you could very quickly reach your burnout point as you struggle to keep up with your assignments. If you feel out of control, ask yourself: are you living out of integrity? It's very possible that you're in a major because you think you should be.

Take a look at your schedule: your classes, extracurriculars, the people you hang out with, etc. Make sure that all of the elements of your life were actually your idea. Where you find incongruencies—things you're doing because someone else thinks you should—take back control.

You sense that circumstances around you are unfair. If you're a member of a marginalized community, college can present a wonderful opportunity to connect with others who share your experience. Perhaps you were judged as a representative of "your group" back at home—you were burdened with the job of finding your own identity while also representing an entire people group to members of the privileged majority who are prone to judge all on the basis of one. That's a heavy load to carry. Maybe you thought things would be different in college—but they're not.

Coming up against racism, anti-Semitism, anti-Islamism, ableism, or any other dehumanizing "ism" is a major blow— especially in college, where people are supposed to be intellectually above all that. If you're encountering "isms," A) I'm so sorry. B) Look and see—is this a one-time incident? Or is it an ugly pattern that's underneath the organization's shiny surface? If the answer is B, choose how you want to engage with that institution. Yet proceed with caution; knocking your head against a brick wall will lead to burnout. Maybe you'd be better off in a more open-minded, welcoming place. You deserve fairness and the chance to be your full self without having to navigate prejudices of the ignorant.

You're not seeing any rewards for your hard work. If you were a big fish in the small pond of high school, you may struggle with receiving few—or zero—external rewards for your efforts in college. Maddy Holleran was accustomed to being number one in track; yet in a college meet, she finished forty-fourth out of one hundred. It was a long way to fall; the reward of finishing at the top was no longer her reality.

Are you accustomed to receiving external rewards that are no longer available to you? If so, try a perspective shift. Practice gratitude for all the good in your life. For instance: if you always got the lead in the high school musical but in college have been relegated to an ensemble member, try being grateful that you *get* to continue participating in an activity that is so meaningful for you. If you enjoy the activity, keep doing it.

Yet maybe you discover that the activities that brought you external rewards no longer bring you joy. If so, it's all right to stop. How can you reward *yourself*? Your rewards may be very simple: for example, commit to studying for two hours, and after your study session take a walk outside with a friend. Choose a way to celebrate the end of a tough semester; plan your celebration in detail and then look forward to your envisioned party every day. When you develop your own internal reward system, you find a way to persevere toward your biggest, most audacious goals—and you have fun along the way.

Your values aren't aligned with your circumstance. We all choose our college and major based on the best information we have at the moment. Perhaps you began college wanting to major in education to positively impact the next generation; yet in college, you're drawn toward business classes. You're attracted to entrepreneurialism and see how entrepreneurs are able to fund initiatives that effect change on a large scale. You feel increasingly frustrated in your education classes—yet you still envision yourself as a teacher, developing the gifts of your students. What do you do?

In situations like this, identifying your values is super important. Which values do you want to guide your life? Values are ideas, like love, freedom, impact, joy, abundance, friendship, and justice. I recommend you spend time learning about your values and then choose your top three. Now do a check-in: are these values reflected in your chosen major? If not, it may be a time for a switch.

Remember: no one's personal values are better or worse than anyone else's. Avoid judging your values and thinking that you *should* value any particular thing. Do a gut check and be true to yourself. Living from your values is another way of saying "having integrity"—you are one *integrated* person, not one person in class, another person with your friends, and someone else with your family. Living with integrity means living with purpose, joy, and freedom. It's worth it.

If you're on the verge of burnout, check and see: Is one of these areas out of order? Be gentle with yourself. Course correct. There is always help available. Find people with whom you can share your burdens and allow those burdens to be lifted. Be more committed to your own happiness than to some ideal of yourself as a "high achiever." It's all right to let go of an old identity in order to find a newer, truer, better one.

REFLECTION QUESTIONS

You've no doubt had your own lemons in life—situations and experiences you didn't choose, yet had to make the best of.

1. What's been the biggest lemon you've encountered thus far?
2. Why was this situation or experience so difficult?
3. Have you made lemonade from it yet?
4. If not, don't worry. Sometimes it takes a while to see the good that comes from a really tough time. Is it possible for you to name just *one* positive that was born from the experience?

Our struggles are not to be ignored. When we persevere through struggle, we gain the strength and resilience we need to accomplish our every dream. Struggles make us, just like joy makes us. Honor your hardships, no matter how painful they've been. Trust that within your hardships are planted the seeds for a beautiful future.

FOURTEEN

Look Back to Look Forward

(Or, How to Figure Out What in the World You Want to Do in Life)

Play is the highest form of research.

—ALBERT EINSTEIN

We've come full circle. In chapter one of this book, "Who Am I?," I asked you to remember who you were as a child. Before the world placed expectations on you, what did you *dream* of for yourself? What was your picture of your future life before *should*s came into the equation? I presented an exercise for you to re-connect with that little kid: here it is again.

Exercise: When I Was Little

1. When I was little, I wanted to grow up to be _____
   _____.

2. That seemed like such a cool thing to be, because ___
   _____.

3. My favorite game to play was _____

_____.

4. As a kid, I was always _____.

5. What got me more excited than anything was when

_____.

6. What I wanted most of all was _____

_____.

7. I wanted to learn more about _____

_____.

Re-connecting with the self of your childhood isn't just something to be done once—it's a practice you can return to again and again. Any time you need guidance, the little kid in you can point the way forward. Here's a secret: we grow older, but we don't grow up. The three-year-old you once were is still inside of you, as is the seven-year-old, the eleven-year-old, the thirteen-year-old . . . etc. That child can be found again, and the quickest way to find them is through *play*.

Remember Jon Youshaei from chapter eleven? In addition to being a YouTube marketing guru, he's also a cartoonist. Every week, more than 100,000 readers enjoy his Every Vowel cartoons, which have been described as "*Dilbert* for millennials" (*Dilbert* is a popular and long-running workplace comic strip that launched in the eighties). Through Every Vowel, Jon gets to share advice on business and life through the medium of cartoons. According to Jon, there's a straight line from his childhood to his side hustle as a cartoonist. Jon's notebooks are filled with his cartoon doodles, scattered among his notes for class. Said Jon: "Your adulthood is a process of rediscovering your childhood. The more you can combine your adulthood and your childhood, the happier you'll be, and the more successful you'll be . . . I think people should think about who they were before the world told them who to be." Jon was "just playing" when he scribbled his childhood doodles—yet in this play existed Jon's deep truth. Your childhood desires—the things you "play" at—provide a map for your future.

In the case of Adrienne Warren, this was literally true. If you haven't heard of Adrienne, she played Tina Turner in *Tina: The Tina Turner Musical*. "Astonishing" is a word that's frequently used to describe Adrienne's performance in the role, which she originated in London's West End and then brought to Broadway in the fall of 2019. One reviewer said of Warren: "She gives an extraordinary, high-octane performance, as dazzling in her tireless vocal and dance duties as she is nuanced in intimate dramatic moments."[1] The role of Tina is one Warren prepared for her entire life.

The person chosen to play Tina Turner had to be a standout athlete. (If you don't know why, search YouTube videos for Tina Turner performances—nonstop cardio, and you have to *sing* while you do it!) Warren, the daughter of a PE teacher, once ran so hard in a 400-meter race that she passed out when she crossed the finish line.[2] In addition, "Tina" had to have "rock and roll" vocal chops—not always easy to be found in performers whose sole background is musical theater. Yet Warren, in addition to musical theater chops, also had experience singing rock and roll: while studying acting in college, Warren joined a rock band and toured with the Trans-Siberian Orchestra. Warren has called playing Tina the biggest challenge of her career; yet her life had prepared her for the role—and her childhood self somehow *knew* it would happen. When Adrienne Warren was a girl, she had a poster on her wall that read: "I want to be the next Tina Turner."[3]

No joke.

When Warren spoke with Tina Turner for the first time, she said: "If it weren't for you, I never would have become a performer. I shook my hips before I could tie my shoes—because of you." Adrienne's father had taught her to sing and introduced her to his musical tastes—from jazz to rock, Elton John to the Rolling Stones. When she discovered Tina Turner, a light switch flicked for Warren. "I had never seen any woman like that. Especially a Black woman."[4]

I think there was power in that poster Warren hung on her wall. It was Warren's little-kid self "calling her shot." There's a famous quote from *The Alchemist*, the well-known allegorical novel by Paulo Coelho about a boy who goes on a quest to find buried treasure: "When you want something, all the Universe conspires in helping you to achieve it." Adrienne Warren couldn't have known that her poster prophecy would come true—just as Jon Youshaei, doodling in his school notebook, couldn't imagine that one day his comics would be read by hundreds of thousands of people around the world. Yet if you believe the quote from *The Alchemist*, the Universe (or God, or Spirit, or whatever you want to call it)—came to their aid. By inhabiting their dreams, Jon and Adrienne were planting seeds. Those seeds would eventually ripen into their destinies.

In chapter one, you re-connected with your inner kid for the purpose of gaining clarity about your college choice. In this chapter, we'll meet luminaries who found the seeds of their future career embedded in their childhood play. Whether you're determining which college you'll attend, your major, where you'll live after college, which job to take, or which person to partner with, whatever juncture you come to, I hope you remember that your little-kid self has much to teach you. If you do what makes the kid happy, *you'll* be happy. It's as simple as that.

. . . .

Larry Namer: Making a Career Out of What Could Be

Larry Namer grew up in the 1960s in a working-class neighborhood in Brooklyn. His parents were not risk-takers; they encouraged Larry to get a civil service job so he could receive a pension. At first Larry thought he would become a teacher—but then the city cut teachers' budgets, and Larry decided to go a different route. At this time, the cable industry was becoming more prominent; Larry observed workers splicing cables on the streets of New York. He was intrigued.

As a child, Larry was always fascinated "not by what is, but by things that could be." Larry said he would play around with science experiments and read voraciously. He'd pick up obscure hobbies, like crocheting. For a short period of time, Larry would read everything he could about his obsession and dive into the hobby; then it would be time to move on to something else.

Larry's restless mind was captivated by cable. As a child, his TV experience consisted of three channels: ABC, NBC, and

CBS. Larry thought: "What if they could make 20 channels?" At the time (before the internet!), imagining 20 channels on television was a major cognitive leap.

Larry went through high school and college as an average to below-average student. His parents didn't know what to make of their son; Larry possessed a keen intellect, yet continued to bring home C grades. Larry was even evaluated by psychologists as his parents strove to understand his sub-par performance. Larry said of school: "I was just bored with it." When it came time to apply to college, all of the schools to which Larry applied rejected him—yet Larry knew that college was for him. He ended up attending Kingsborough Community College for two years and transferring to Brooklyn College, where Larry earned his degree in economics.

The "normal" career path for someone with an economics degree is to climb the ladder in a white-collar job. Yet Larry didn't see himself pursuing that life. Larry began his career on the operations side of the cable industry; he was an assistant to the underground splicer. It was hardly a glamorous role; Larry worked under the streets of New York, splicing cable among rats and cockroaches.

Most of the people Larry worked with didn't even have a high school diploma. They were amazed at Larry's aptitude; Larry could read the manuals and learn the material quickly. Because of his unique skill set, Larry assumed more and more responsibilities and leadership roles. He was promoted from service technician to installer to advanced technician. Larry moved into a management position with 300 people reporting to him at the age of 25. Most of his colleagues in management came from white-collar backgrounds and Ivy League schools; they had no knowledge of the technical side of the cable industry, which Larry had mastered.

Larry rose to the role of vice president at Manhattan Cable. At the time, Manhattan was the only place in the world that had underground cable. As more cities began to acquire cable franchises, they needed people who knew how to build cable systems underground. Larry was recruited by a company in California to oversee the building of their cable system—and offered *four times* what he was making in New York. Larry couldn't refuse.

The company that recruited Larry was based in Canada—soon after Larry moved, they decided to sell their U.S. interests. He could keep his job . . . if he moved to Canada. Larry saw an opportunity: he thought, "I've always wanted to go out on my own, and I'll probably never get this chance again." Larry had an idea for a new television network. This was audacious—back then, only corporations (not individuals) launched TV networks. Yet Larry was excited by his idea to launch the "MTV of movie channels." He and a partner drew up a business plan and set about the task of enlisting investors. Three and a half years later, what would eventually become E! Entertainment Television was launched. Today, E! is valued at over $4 *billion*.

LESSONS FROM LARRY'S STORY

- **You're the only person who needs to understand your choices.**

- (Ahem: does this point sound familiar? We talked about this one when we met Ezina in chapter twelve. The point bears repeating! Be sure you can explain your choices to yourself. Other people can weigh in on your life—but you get the final say.)
- Larry was misunderstood from an early age. His parents couldn't understand why Larry's performance in school was so underwhelming; Larry was evaluated and tested relentlessly, when the truth about his lackluster grades was much simpler than a complex diagnosis: boredom. After college, Larry once again followed a track that could have left many scratching their heads. He graduated from a four-year college with a fancy economics degree . . . to work underground with cockroaches and rats?
- Larry had an aversion to the expected path of a white-collar job—so he chose a path that worked for him. He was less concerned about what others would think than about following his own instinct. To the outside world, it may have appeared as if Larry was slacking off. I don't think so; I think the little boy inside Larry—the one who'd always been fascinated by cable—made the decision for him. Larry's actions did not appear like a good career move; he could not have known that splicing cables underground was *exactly* the experience he would need to ascend to the heights of a cable corporation and one day be a successful media entrepreneur. You don't have to see the whole path:

in fact, if you *could*, you'd probably be overwhelmed. All you have to know is what feels better and what feels worse. Move in the direction of better.

- **There's no such thing as an overnight success.** When Larry worked to get his movie network off the ground, people didn't understand his vision. While the going rate to start a network was around $60 million, Larry and his business partners could only raise $2.5 million. They launched the network anyway along with 30 interns and 11 employees. And yet when the network premiered, people got it. They said: "Why didn't you tell us this was what you wanted to do? We would have given you money." Said Larry: "We were a three-and-a-half-year overnight success."

- Hear this: there is no such thing as an overnight success. From the outside looking in, things can sometimes appear to magically work out for someone—as if they speak the word, and BOOM! Everything lines up perfectly for them. In truth, we're only seeing the tip of the iceberg. Underneath the water lies everything we *don't* see: the countless rejections, close calls, deals that fell through, people who unexpectedly backed out of the project, health setbacks, periods of depression ... etc. David Heinemeier Hansson, a Danish entrepreneur, has a quote about the phenomenon of sudden success: "Nobody is an overnight success. Most overnight successes you see have been working at it for ten years."

- Have no fear if your grand ideas don't materialize after one year . . . or two, or three, or even ten. Keep going. When the success you're seeking comes, you'll be ready for it.
- **Find the evidence that says it's possible.** When Larry decided to start his network, the idea was radical. Conventional wisdom said that individuals didn't start networks—corporations did. And yet, Larry was able to point to evidence that proved individuals *could* start networks. Robert Johnson had recently launched BET, and John Hendricks had launched the Discovery Channel. Larry looked at this evidence and thought: "Why not me?" He set to work creating a business plan.
- If you've got a goal that seems impossible—that others say can't be achieved—chances are, someone somewhere has already done it. Instead of listening to the naysayers, give your attention to the people who are living your dream. Look at their results and work backward. How did they get where they are? Who did they connect with? What kind of experience did they need in order to be in their current position?
- Like Larry, choose to focus on what could be instead of what is. If you ask better questions, you'll get better answers. Instead of finding evidence that something is impossible, ask yourself the questions: "Why not?" and "Why not me?"

. . . .

Katlyn Grasso: Entrepreneur from Childhood

Katlyn Grasso has a seriously impressive resume. As of this writing, she's a few years shy of 30; yet Katlyn has already founded several companies, including GenHERation. GenHERation is a network where young women and companies connect through their digital platform and national events. Since 2014, GenHERation has empowered more than 400,000 young women and hosted 500 events across North America, including their widely recognized Discovery Days— the largest career exploration trip for young women in North America. Katlyn was selected by *Seventeen* magazine as a "Seventeen Power Girl" and was named to the magazine's list of "Real Girls Doing Amazing Things." Katlyn speaks nationally about entrepreneurship, technology, and women's advancement and has been featured in numerous national radio and television broadcasts. Katlyn has started two nonprofit organizations: the dance exercise program Tap for Tots and a technology commercialization venture. Business and entrepreneurship are in Katlyn's blood.

Yet Katlyn began college as a pre-med major.

Growing up in Buffalo, Katlyn didn't have many examples of successful entrepreneurs around her. She aspired to attend the Ivy League, because she knew she was destined for something *big*—yet no one in her sphere set their sights on entrepreneurship. Katlyn attended an informational session for Wharton and was captivated; the representative said, "If you want business and more, then Wharton is the place for you!"

According to Katlyn, it was like a light came down from the ceiling. She knew she *had* to go to Wharton. Katlyn loved business; in Girl Scouts, she started two nonprofits to earn her Silver and Gold awards, and she had always enjoyed making and selling things. Katlyn was a born entrepreneur, before she even knew what an entrepreneur was.

Katlyn knew this about herself—it's why she was so insistent on attending Wharton. And yet she felt the need to hedge her bets. Despite her driving passion for business and her success in establishing nonprofits, Katlyn wasn't surrounded by successful models of entrepreneurship. She'd grown up with the understanding that becoming a doctor was the "mecca of success." So, Katlyn decided to become a pre-med major in case the businesses didn't work out.

One day, Katlyn found herself in her pre-med lab, measuring the electrolyte concentration of Gatorade, and thought to herself, "What am I doing?" Katlyn was putting in a *ton* of work on a career path that wasn't her true calling. (I don't need to tell you that being a doctor isn't exactly an easy fallback plan!) That moment in the lab was life-changing for Katlyn. She decided to let go of others' ideas of success and pursue her own vision.

But Katlyn had to let go of her own ideas, too. She'd told lots of people that she was going to be a doctor. That was the "respectable" path, after all. Yet Katlyn realized: "This is not fun for me, this is not my purpose in life. Let's re-write the plan." And that's what she did.

LESSONS FROM KATLYN'S STORY

- **Everyone's definition of *normal* is different. Live your own.** In Katlyn's environment, most people stayed close to her hometown of Buffalo, New York. A pre-professional route that prepared someone to be a doctor or lawyer was the ultimate ambitious plan. What's the norm where you live? What vocations are prized?

- Maybe everyone in your family becomes an engineer or teacher. Maybe you come from a family of academics and talk about achieving tenure and taking sabbaticals around the dinner table. What professions are within reach? What professions are slightly out of reach? Everyone's version of *normal* and *ambitious* is different. These are arbitrary designations and have a lot to do with what your parents do, where you live, the culture of your high school, what your teachers encourage you to reach for, and so on. These designations don't matter—your desires *do*. Yet it's helpful to know what the expectations of others are—that way, you can weed out cultural norms from your own wants. And the best way to re-connect with your own desires is to go back to childhood and see what you enjoyed doing *then*. For Katlyn, it's always been entrepreneurship: making things and selling them. What's the "thing" for you?

- **Let go of perfectionism.** Katlyn said that in high school, she was the type of kid who'd get a 99 on a math test and then chase down the teacher, wanting to know where she'd gone wrong and how she could get a 100 next time. (Know anyone like that? Is that you?) Yet as an entrepreneur, Katlyn *can't* let perfectionism slow her down. There are too many decisions to make and too many people to be managed. Everything works in service to the larger goal of GenHERation: connecting young women to exciting career opportunities. Katlyn can't worry about perfectionism: there are too many people to serve!

- Perfectionism can serve you very well when you're trying to get *in* to college. I hate to admit it, but it's true. (Of course, as we've already discussed, a perfect GPA and test scores are not the *only* things that will serve you well: admissions committees are much more interested in seeing you as a three-dimensional person with opinions and interests that you express and explore.) Yet in college and after, *you don't have time* for perfectionism. There's too much to do in your journey to become who you are.

- Perfectionism will have you constantly looking over your shoulder—"Who's doing better? Who's doing worse? Person XYZ got this prestigious award from our department—why wasn't it me?" Perfectionism will get you into the weeds and leave you stuck there: part of growing up is letting it go. Determine your own personal standards and make sure you're upholding them. Worry about disappointing yourself, but don't stress over meeting some nebulous standard of perfection. Perfection doesn't exist.

- **No two success journeys look alike.** When Katlyn was nearing college graduation, her friends were talking about what "real jobs" they were going to get. Katlyn hadn't even considered getting a "real job," though that's what you're "supposed" to do after college. Conventional wisdom says: get a job, get experience for a few years, and then make your next move—whether that's up the corporate ladder or on to something else.

- Yet in truth, Katlyn already had "real-world" job experience. Katlyn began working at Wharton's Small Business Development Center (SBDC), a pro bono consulting firm that works with companies that supported multimillion-dollar businesses. Katlyn started working there her sophomore year; by her junior year, she was the managing practice leader. She had 50 students, undergraduate and graduate, reporting to her . . . as a 19-year-old, Katlyn had 35-year-old MBAs looking to her for leadership! Katlyn's time at SBDC taught her an enormous amount and deepened her passion for entrepreneurship. Surely, that experience would be impressive on a resume in an application for a "real job."

- But jumping into a corporate job didn't ring true for Katlyn, a born entrepreneur—and she's done just fine without one. Don't buy into any "supposed tos";

you may see your peers taking what seems to them the logical next step after college, yet you may feel pulled in a completely different direction. That's perfectly fine. Try this thought on for size: "Anything that follows *should* is a lie." If you tell yourself you *should* do this or that, stop and examine the thought. Dig deeper; find the desire that's buried beneath the *should* and listen to that instead.

REFLECTION QUESTIONS

It's time to check in with your little-kid self again. Grab your journal and try the following exercises:

1. Brainstorm all the things you did as a kid that made you happy. Don't censor yourself—write down whatever pops into your mind, even if it seems mundane (ex: "I threw my ball against the side of the house all afternoon."). Only write down things that truly brought your kid-self joy; get as much as you can on paper. Now, look over your list.

    What could you do right now to re-capture that carefree feeling? Let's say you wrote down "picking honeysuckles." Is it honeysuckle season? Grab a friend, head outside, and hunt down the nearest honeysuckle bush. You'll be amazed at how quickly your kid self comes rushing back to you. Whenever you need to connect with her, go back to this list and pick an activity. Keep your relationship with your little-kid self alive and well; learn everything they have to teach you.

2. Write a letter to your current self from your kid self. What was your favorite year of elementary school? Choose that year. What did that kid like and not like? What does that kid have to say to you as a young adult? If you want to take this one step further, write a letter as an 80-year-old to your current self. What does the *older* you have to teach you?[5]

Your little-kid self encourages you to have fun and not take everything so seriously. Childhood is about play. Re-capturing that sense of play is the journey we're all on—so we can, in the words of Jon Youshaei, combine our childhood and adulthood. When we do this, we don't leave fun behind on the elementary school playground—life becomes more and more fun the older we get.

And who doesn't want that?

College Is Just the Beginning

Your education is a dress rehearsal
for a life that is yours to lead.

—NORA EPHRON

Congratulations! You've reached the end of this book. My hope is that you now understand that what your version of success looks like is entirely up to *you*. I hope you're learning to let go of what others expect and follow the path that is authentic and aligned with your personality and interests. I hope you've loosened your grip on *should*s; that you've realized *everyone* has their own unique path, and the best you can do at each twist and turn in the journey is to follow your instinct. You never know where one step will lead, and you can't see the entire path in front of you. Just press on, following your curiosity.

Consider this chapter my commencement address to you. At college commencement ceremonies, a celebrated figure imparts wisdom to the graduating class. They share what they've learned along the way, offering funny and profound insights to those about to embark on the rest of their lives. Here, I leave you with parting reflections meant to encourage, motivate, comfort, and inspire you as you reach for greatness.

College graduation ceremonies are a time of intense emotion and introspection. They provide a moment to look back and celebrate all you've accomplished in your school years. Some arrive at college graduation with a clear idea of their next step: med school starts in the fall, they start their first "grown-up" job in the summer, they're going to grad school, etc. For many others, college graduation feels like stepping off a ladder. They've climbed the ladder for so long—from kindergarten to high school to college. Each next rung has been right there waiting for them; moving up the ladder has required little thought. Up through college, the steps have been pre-ordained: select next semester's classes, register, get your books, show up in class, and do your best. What happens when there's no "next semester" on the horizon? When you realize that your life is truly your own creation . . . how do you shape it?

The thought can be overwhelming. You graduate college with *so much* of your life left to live. How do you even begin to take steps in the direction of your future? What happens if you make a wrong move? Wouldn't it be so much easier if you could see it all—if someone held a crystal ball that showed you exactly what to do?

Whether you're certain of your next step after college or not, know this: no one *really* knows what their future holds. If you're an extreme type-A planner, this news may freak you out—but it's not meant to. Since no one *really* knows anything, there's no such thing as a wrong move. The person who's certain about going to law school may get one semester in and realize they hate it. Then what? The clueless graduate could move home with Mom and Dad, re-connect with a mentor from childhood, and suddenly be turned on to a career path that becomes their life's work. *None of us knows what the future holds.* The key is to stay open and optimistic. You don't have to live your whole life at once: you only have to live this moment, this day. If you're continually turning toward the ideas, activities, and people that light you up, eventually you'll create a life that satisfies you on every level.

One of my favorite commencement addresses ever was given by Conan O'Brien to the Dartmouth graduating class of 2011. (Look it up on YouTube—it's inspiring *and* hilarious.) Conan gave his speech in the aftermath of a public career humiliation. As a comedian, Conan had always aspired to host *The Tonight Show.* This gig was considered the pinnacle of success for comedians of his generation. In 2004, a public plan was laid out by which Conan would take over *The Tonight Show* from the show's then host, Jay Leno. During the transition in 2009 with Conan as host, the show's ratings started slipping with older viewers. As a result, NBC wanted to retain both Conan O'Brien and Jay Leno. NBC proposed a plan: Jay Leno would resume hosting a show at 11:35 p.m., *The Tonight Show*'s time slot; Conan would be moved back to his former 12:35 p.m. time slot. Conan and his team refused—as a result, he was off the air and on the outs with NBC, which had been his professional home for 17 years.

The firing was deeply disillusioning to Conan, who'd

worked his entire career in comedy with the goal of one day hosting *The Tonight Show*. Anyone would be distraught to have their dream job snatched from their grasp—and for Conan, the "snatching" happened in front of millions of viewers. But then, things began to shift for Conan:

> *Fogbound, with no compass, and adrift, I started trying things . . . I dove into the world of social media. I started tweeting my comedy. I threw together a national tour. I played the guitar. I did stand-up, wore a skin-tight blue leather suit, recorded an album, made a documentary, and frightened my friends and family.*
>
> *Ultimately, I abandoned all preconceived perceptions of my career path . . . I did a lot of silly, unconventional, spontaneous and seemingly irrational things and guess what: with the exception of the blue leather suit, it was the most satisfying and fascinating year of my professional life.*[1]

Conan assured the Dartmouth graduates that your path at 22 will not be what it is at 32 or 42 . . . your dreams and vision for your life are constantly evolving: "Whatever you think your dream is now, it will probably change. And that's okay." Conan said that no specific job or career goal defines him. Career disappointments may come, but no disappointment is the end of the road; we can respond to our changing circumstances with curiosity and courage. Then, the perceived failures are transformed into the seeds of our next great re-invention.

I hope you've gotten that message loud and clear in the pages of this book. Failure is only failure if you stop there: if you keep going, you will transform that failure into success. Think of Henry Louis Gates Jr., who dreamed of attending an Ivy League university yet got cold feet and returned to his home in West Virginia after attending Exeter, a prestigious prep school. Henry applied for re-admission, and Exeter said no. Yet this wasn't failure; Henry kept his Ivy League dreams alive and applied for a transfer to Yale during his sophomore year of college. It worked: Henry got in.

Remember Aaron Kirman, who was kicked out of his university's ROTC program and later fired from his first real estate job? Both experiences taught Aaron about himself. He learned that he was unsuited to the military and unhappy in the ROTC, even if it meant free college. Then, Aaron learned that he was capable of earning the money needed to pay back his college loans. After getting fired, Aaron learned that he didn't want to work for someone else. Each experience planted the seeds for Aaron's evolution into a billion-dollar real estate entrepreneur.

Conan put it this way: "It is our failure to become our perceived ideal that ultimately defines us and makes us unique." This is how it so often works: we try to be someone else, fail, and end up becoming more ourselves. I'm glad this was true in my own life—that I'm not still trying to live up to my ideal of a music business professional—and have instead found the path I'm on today. Ezina LeBlanc, whom we met in chapter twelve, "failed" at becoming a lawyer and instead became an electrifying musician and businesswoman whose art has touched audiences around the globe.

In the final pages of this book, I want to introduce you to

one more luminary who has wisdom to offer as you go out into the world. Raya Bidshahri is the founder and chief executive officer of Awecademy, an online educational platform that offers global learners the chance to learn, connect, and solve humanity's grand challenges. A voracious reader and writer, Raya writes about the societal and existential implications of accelerating technology on our species. Raya has been described by the media and those who know her as a futurist, a techno optimist, a communicator of popular science, and an advocate of curiosity, critical thinking, wonder, and awe.

Raya spoke to me about the uncertainty of the future job market and the futility of trying to predict what exact skills people will need in order to "get ahead" professionally. She watches many students struggle as they try to plot out their careers. Said Raya: "We know that a majority of jobs of the future don't even exist yet, because new industries are constantly being born and old ones are dying out." Raya's Awecademy helps students think outside the box to meet the demands of an unknown future. Lessons are multidisciplinary and focus on topics that are not covered in traditional education: for instance, learners can explore modules that cover finding your passion and purpose, artificial intelligence, ethics, exponential thinking, twenty-first-century ethics, ethics of the future, and living on Mars. To Raya, this approach makes a lot more sense than pressuring students to choose their career paths as young adults. Raya believes that young people should be given guidance and mentorship as they discern their paths but that they should also be free to *change their minds* often. She encourages young people to be comfortable with uncertainty. Said Raya: "The future *isn't* set in stone in so many ways. *We're creating the future*" (emphasis mine). To that end, don't worry about trying to fit yourself into any type of box based on your thoughts about where the world will be in the next 5, 10, or 20 years. The best you can do is figure out who *you* are, and then seize opportunities that excite you. Look for, as Frederick Buechner put it, the place where "your deep gladness and the world's deep hunger meet." When we find this sweet spot, our work becomes a joy.

I love the phrase "deep gladness," because it reminds me that *my* joy is a priority. So often, we lose sight of this. We get overcome by *should*s. Katlyn Grasso thought she *should* be a doctor because it's a prestigious role and was the ultimate example of a successful person when she was a child. Not only are physicians respected—they also save lives. Who would argue with someone who's thinking of becoming a doctor? No one! So, Katlyn became a pre-med major.

Yet medicine was not where Katlyn's deep gladness lay. Her heart belonged to entrepreneurship—even though getting people on board with entrepreneurship is a harder sell than saying you want to be a pediatrician. Yet others' perceptions of your path are not what count. Don't ask: "What will my aunt think of this?" or "What about all those people I told I was pursuing pre-med?" What counts is your ability to *live with your own choices*. If your choices aren't giving you a sense of deep gladness, it's time to re-examine them and choose a path that feels better.

If you're having trouble remembering the things that bring

you deep gladness, look back through your childhood. Think about what excited you then. For hours at a time, Larry Namer would watch workers splicing cables on the New York City streets. Little did he know that those workers were *literally* laying the foundation for his future career. Henry Louis Gates Jr. was fascinated by his own family history, his "estimable" great-great-great-grandmother. He'd stumbled on the seeds of his career as an academic and researcher of African American history. Joshua Habermann combined his lifelong love of languages and music into choral conducting, a career that combines the two. What were your childhood passions? How can you, as Jon Youshaei put it, make your adulthood look like your childhood?

As Jon did on his first trip to Penn, stay open for moments of fate in which new doors open and new worlds become available. Had he not connected with the dynamic tour guide—who later became a valued friend and business partner—things may have looked very differently for Jon. Joshua Habermann, in a moment of open-heartedness, suddenly realized that music needed to be his vocation. Joshua acted on that impulse, even though he was about to graduate with a degree in a different field. He didn't put off the next right action for "someday"; Joshua went to his teachers and mentors and told them about his new direction. From there, Joshua and his teachers took the inspired action needed to set him up for a career in music. He stepped off his path—but a new path appeared. When we're open to guidance from forces greater than ourselves, that is what happens.

Remember: your journey will not be pain free. Life is

guaranteed to hand you some lemons. It's up to you to decide what to make of them. Remember Bethany, the former client I introduced you to in chapter four? She did not let her chronic illness limit her expectations. Bethany chose to *use* her chronic illness; through it, she learned how to better appreciate life. Bethany also learned to trust herself; she knew her limits and capabilities better than anyone, so if she received advice on how to manage her illness that wasn't in alignment with her truth, Bethany could set that advice aside. Laura Orrico from chapter thirteen allowed a devastating experience—the death of her husband—to plant the seeds for a new career in public relations. Laura relied on her natural gifts for connection and her late husband's belief in her abilities; she was able to identify a problem (entertainers' needs for PR services, their uncertainty about where to find them) and fill it in her own unique way. Thus, Laura launched her second act.

No hardship, however difficult, is the end of the road for you. No matter what obstacles you face, remember that there is always help available. Seek support from trusted adults, friends, and professionals. Know that you have a big purpose on this earth—a mission to fulfill. It's all right if you don't know what it is, or if clouds obscure your vision from time to time. Just remember: *we need you*. We need your laughter, your joy, your sadness, your creativity, your solutions, your kindness, your wittiness, your *you*-ness. You are part of the whole, connected to everyone and everything on earth. You make this planet better just by existing; please keep on shining your light.

Exercise: Writing Your Manifesto

To conclude this book, I invite you to write your personal manifesto. Merriam-Webster defines *manifesto* as "a written statement declaring publicly the intentions, motives, or views of its issuer." Writing your own manifesto means writing out your ideals and wishes for your life, and then rephrasing those as if they're *already true*. Here's how you do it:

1. Write down a list of your aspirations and dreams. What do you want to be good at? What behaviors are important to you? What do you value? What are your highest ideals for your career?

2. As a start, you may write something like this:
   I want to be a leader. I want to positively impact others that I meet and leave everyone smiling. I want to help the earth and find positive solutions to the environmental crisis. I want to make responsible choices in my life and career that will help the next generation and the one after that.

3. Your list can be much longer; this is just an example. Make your list as long as you like—write down everything you can think of that's truly important to you.

4. Now, re-write your list using affirmative sentences. The above paragraph could become:
   I am a leader. I positively impact everyone I meet. Everywhere I go, I make people smile. I am part of the solution to the global environmental crisis. I make responsible

choices in my life and business that help the earth now,
and for many generations to come.

5. Now you're moving from the "I want" energy to the "I AM" energy. *To manifest* means to make evident or certain by showing or displaying. When you read your manifesto with its affirmations of the life you want to create, you are creating that life *as you speak it*. You are not looking toward some ideal future; you're *creating* that future with your words. That's why it's important to be as detailed as possible! If you can write your vision down and perceive it as real, it will be.

6. Now make a clean copy of your manifesto and put it someplace where you can't miss it—perhaps your bedside table or bathroom mirror. Re-read your manifesto every day. I recommend you read it out loud!

7. The more you can connect with the energy and excitement behind your words, the faster you will create your dream life. Come back often to this place of certainty. Here, creative solutions to your problems will appear; your right next step will always be shown. Your vision will guide you to everything you need to know.

I believe that you are more capable than you can imagine. You are a powerful force on this planet. College can help shape you into the most authentic version of yourself, but that work is ongoing. The work of becoming you is not the work of four years: it's the work of a lifetime. "Getting real" is a wild adventure, full of twists and turns and bumps along the way—but it's *worth it*. In the words of poet Mary Oliver, we all have "one wild and precious life"; what we do with it is our gift to the world.

I can't wait to see what you do with yours.

Acknowledgments

This book was conceived, born, and changed over the course of five years. It is in your hands today because of the support of my incredible family, friends, and colleagues.

First, I have to thank my husband, Joel Legatt. Joel's positive and steadfast support allowed me to have the time, space, and foundation to get this book created and published. Joel is an incredible teacher in the city of Philadelphia and provided helpful perspective on kids. He also does a lot of cooking for me and the family to make sure we're well nourished. Thank you, Joel. You're simply the best in every way.

To my sons, Jarron and Micah. Although you have no idea what Mommy is up to, your smiles and youthful optimism are a buoying force. Thank you.

To my parents, Harriet and Jeff. Thank you for making sacrifices so that I could follow my dreams and be myself. Appreciate and love you always.

To my in-laws, Liz and Alan. You are role models of

balancing ambition with empathy. Thank you for your support of our family and for your support of my professional adventures.

To my BFFs from high school, Celia and Ann. I learned so much about the world from you as a kid, which has shaped me into the woman I am today. Celia, if we hadn't pored over those college books for so many hours complemented by our note-passing and endless phone conversations, I don't know if this book would have happened. Ann, thank you for tutoring me, for being a brick wall, and for being a model of resilience and hard work. Heeeeeeyyyyy!

To my network of friends from PHS, NYU, and Penn, I think of you through this book—much of my real education happened outside of the classroom and within the company of your excellence.

To my group of amazing mentors and friends: with special thanks to Caroline Stokes, my book mentor and professional fairy godmother, and Dorie Clark, who opened up an incredible network and new professional doors that I didn't know existed. Much love also to Marie Incontrera, Alisa Cohn, Marlena Corcoran, Sher Downing, Laura Gassner Otting, and the REx network. Thank you for being such beautiful examples of powerful and giving women. You are my professional compasses. Has anyone ever told you that you are "so RExy"?

Thank you to Adam Grant for his early support of this book, including his endorsement, participating in an interview, and his book marketing tips. I have no doubt that

Adam's support helped open doors that may have otherwise been shut. Thank you so much, Adam.

Thank you to the interviewees in this book. Your stories are timeless and potent. You are a wonderful example to readers. Thank you for sharing your stories from growing up, a lovely window into your being.

Thank you to my incredible team at Ivy Insight, including Amy, Josh, Linda, Mandee, and many others. Your dedication elevates our students, families, and the transformative work we get to be involved in. Thank you for everything.

Thank you to St. Martin's Press, especially Kevin Reilly, who helped me carry the torch and make my dream come true, and Lauren Jablonski, who first championed the book. Kevin, you helped me navigate this world of publishing with patience and support. Your kindness and candor were incredibly helpful in making sure the book was as good as it could be. Lauren, you helped me make sure that the book proposal was something worth buying. Your championing and mentorship, no doubt, helped me get this deal. Thank you both, dearly. Thanks to the St. Martin's team at large behind the scenes, including Anne Marie Tallberg, Paul Hochman, Sara Beth Haring, Sara LaCotti, Jessica Zimmerman, and Jennifer Fernandez.

Thank you to Jennifer Locke, who tirelessly worked with me on early book drafts to make sure that they were as polished, clear, and YA-friendly as possible. I couldn't have sounded as cool without Jennifer's perspective. Thank you.

To the students who I work with year after year on the

college process, this book would not have happened without you. I love working with you and I can't wait to watch you grow in high school, college, and beyond. Cheers to your success (however you define that) and, most importantly, life satisfaction.

Notes

A resource guide featuring some of the exercises in this book (and more) is available at www.getrealandgetin.com; see also the Resources list on page 247.

Introduction: The Impressiveness Paradox

1 M. K. Eagan et al., "The American Freshman: Fifty-Year Trends, 1966–2015," Higher Education Research Institute, University of California, Los Angeles, 2016.

2 Thomas Espenshade, Lauren Hale, and Chang Chung, "The Frog Pond Revisited: High School Academic Context, Class Rank, and Elite College Admission," *Sociology of Education* 78 (2005): 269–293.

3 R. Lent et al., "Toward a Unifying Social Cognitive Theory of Career and Academic Interest, Choice, and Performance," *Journal of Vocational Behavior* 45, no. 1 (1994): 79–122.

One: Who Am I?

1 This exercise is adapted from author and executive coach Ron Carucci's work: Ron Carucci, "Getting to the Bottom of Destructive Behaviors," *Harvard Business Review*, December 9, 2019,

available at https://hbr.org/2019/12/getting-to-the-bottom-of
-destructive-behaviors.

Two: What Do I Want?

1 Dan Buettner, "How to Live to Be 100+," TEDxTC, September
2009, available at https://www.ted.com/talks/dan_buettner_how
_to_live _to_be_100.
2 "Beginning College Students Who Change Their Majors
Within 3 Years of Enrollment," Data Point, U.S. Department of
Education, NCES 2018–434, December 2017, https://nces.ed
.gov/pubs2018/2018434.pdf.
3 "Employee Tenure Summary," U.S. Bureau of Labor Statistics,
September 22, 2020, available at https://www.bls.gov/news
.release/tenure.nr0.htm.
4 "STEM OPT Hub," U.S. Department of Homeland Security,
available at https://studyinthestates.dhs.gov/stem-opt-hub/stem
-opt-extension-overview.
5 Jean M. Twenge, Thomas E. Joiner, Megan L. Rogers, et al., "Increases in Depressive Symptoms, Suicide-Related Outcomes,
and Suicide Rates Among U.S. Adolescents After 2010 and
Links to Increased New Media Screen Time," *Clinical Psychological Science* 6, no. 1 (January 2018), available at https://journals
.sagepub.com/doi/full/10.1177/2167702617723376.

Three: Dare to Dream

1 Adam Grant biography, available at https://www.adamgrant.net
/about/biography/.

Five: Know Your Needs

1 Per payscale.com, October 18, 2020, available at https://www
.payscale.com/research/US/Job=Journalist/Salary.

2 Per *U.S. News and World Report*, October 18, 2020, available at https://www.usnews.com/best-colleges/california-state-university -sacramento-1150.

3 "The State of LD: Understanding the 1 in 5," National Center for Learning Disabilities, May 2, 2017, available at https://www .ncld.org/news/newsroom/the-state-of-ld-understanding-the-1 -in-5.

4 Catherine Gewertz, "Why Don't Students Apply for Financial Aid?," *Education Week*, December 19, 2018, available at https:// www.edweek.org/teaching-learning/why-dont-students-apply- for-financial-aid/2018/12.

5 "CSS Profile," College Board, available at https://cssprofile .collegeboard.org/.

Eight: Go Big or Go Home

1 "Best-Selling Author Elizabeth Gilbert on Finding the Cour- age to Live a Creative Life," corporate.target.com, February 3, 2017, available at https://corporate.target.com/article/2017/02 /liz-gilbert-outer-spaces.

2 Paul Franz, "Give Teens More Downtime and Support With Time Management," *ASCD Express* 14, no. 26 (May 9, 2019), available at http://www.ascd.org/ascd-express/vol14/num26/give -teens-more-downtime-and-support-with-time-management .aspx.

3 Jean M. Twenge, Thomas E. Joiner, Megan L. Rogers, et al., "Increases in Depressive Symptoms, Suicide-Related Out- comes, and Suicide Rates Among U.S. Adolescents After 2010 and Links to Increased New Media Screen Time," *Clinical Psy- chological Science* 6, no. 1 (January 2018), available at https:// journals.sagepub.com/doi/full/10.1177/2167702617723376.

Eleven: Be Open to the New

1 Jeremy Bowers et al., "The Best Commencement Speeches, Ever," NPR.org, May 19, 2014, last updated July 2, 2015, available at https://apps.npr.org/commencement/.

Twelve: Chart Your Own Path

1 "Wesleyan University Hamilton Prize," Wesleyan University, available at https://www.wesleyan.edu/admission/apply/hamiltonprize .html.

2 Peter Marks, "'Hamilton' Director, Thomas Kail, at the Height of His Powers," *Washington Post*, July 31, 2015, available at https://www.washingtonpost.com/entertainment/theater_dance /hamilton-director-thomas-kail-at-the-height-of-his-powers /2015/07/30/4be3e08a-2e3c-11e5–8f36–18d1d501920d_story .html.

Thirteen: Turn Lemons Into Lemonade

1 Elizabeth Scott, "Burnout Symptoms and Treatment," *Very Well Mind*, March 20, 2020, available at https://www.verywellmind .com/stress-and-burnout-symptoms-and-causes-3144516.

2 Elizabeth Grace Saunders, "6 Causes of Burnout, and How to Avoid Them," *Harvard Business Review*, July 5, 2019, available at https://hbr.org/2019/07/6-causes-of-burnout-and-how-to-avoid -them.

Fourteen: Look Back to Look Forward

1 *Hollywood Reporter* staff, "'Tina: The Tina Turner Musical': Theater Review," *Hollywood Reporter*, November 7, 2019, available at https://www.hollywoodreporter.com/review/tina-tina-turner -musical-theater-review-1253132.

2   Naveen Kumar, "From Annie to Tina Turner, and Trained to Go
    the Distance," *New York Times*, October 30, 2019, available at
    https://www.nytimes.com/2019/10/30/theater/adrienne-warren
    -tina-turner-broadway-musical.html.
3   TINA The Musical Shorts, episode 3, "Adrienne Warren's TINA
    Journey," YouTube.com, March 19, 2018, available at https://
    www.youtube.com/watch?v=bjMKffiZtMo.
4   Kumar, "From Annie to Tina Turner, and Trained to Go the
    Distance."
5   Exercise adapted from Julia Cameron, *The Artist's Way* (New
    York: J. P. Tarcher/Putnam), 2002.

Conclusion: College Is Just the Beginning

1   For a full video of the commencement speech, see Mark Mem-
    mott, "Did Conan O'Brien Give 'The Greatest Commence-
    ment Speech Ever'?," NPR, June 16, 2011, https://www.npr
    .org/sections/thetwo-way/2011/06/16/137218460/did-conan
    -obrien-give-the-greatest-commencement-speech-ever.

Resources

- Additional stories and resources from this book at www.getrealandgetin.com
- Have a question for Dr. Legatt? Text "book" to 610-222-5762
- Dr. Aviva Legatt's social media: Facebook, Instagram, Twitter, LinkedIn: @avivalegatt
  TikTok: @collegeadmissionstips
- Podcast: *College Admissions Real Talk* available on iTunes, Libysyn and YouTube
- For one-to-one college admissions advice, visit www.ivyinsight.com

Index